A Pastor's
Practical Guide
to Funerals

Offering Help, Assurance, and Hope

Lee Franklin

Abingdon Press
Nashville

A PASTOR'S PRACTICAL GUIDE TO FUNERALS:
OFFERING HELP, ASSURANCE, AND HOPE

This book is printed on acid-free paper.

Library of Congress Cataloging-in-Publication Data has been requested.

ISBN 978-1-4267-5819-5

Scripture quotations are taken from the New Revised Standard Version of the Bible, copyright 1989, Division of Christian Education of the National Council of the Churches of Christ in the United States of America. Used by permission. All rights reserved.

Disclaimer: Names and significant details of individuals have been changed by the author to protect their identities.

13 14 15 16 17 18 19 20 21 22—10 9 8 7 6 5 4 3 2 1

MANUFACTURED IN THE UNITED STATES OF AMERICA

To Warren

CONTENTS

Acknowledgments vii

Introduction ix

Chapter 1: Preparing for Death 1

Chapter 2: Caring through Anticipated Death 19

Chapter 3: Caring through Sudden Death 33

Chapter 4: Meeting with Family before the Funeral Service 53

Chapter 5: Creating the Funeral Service 71

Chapter 6: Creating the Funeral Sermon 93

Chapter 7: Following Up with Grievers 113

Appendix 133

Notes 153

Suggested Reading 159

Acknowledgments

I wish to thank three people in particular for their careful and thoughtful contributions to this book and beyond: Lindell Anderson, Warren Carter, and Tom Reeder. Without them, this book would not be possible.

I also wish to thank the following people for their contributions to this book: Rabbi Jonathan Kligler; pastors Jeff Clayton, Katherine Godby, Mike Graves, Jim Gordon, Katie Hays, Meg Peery McLaughlin, Holly McKissick, George Moore, Rob Morris, Tom Plumbley, Tom Reeder, and Ginger Watson; chaplains Lindell Anderson, Robert Beltram, and Khalebb Ramirez; and Elder Linda King. Their compelling funeral ministry is abundantly evident in chapters 5 and 6. I greatly appreciate their willingness to share their work. I am also grateful for conversations with and resources from Dr. Harold Ivan Smith. Special thanks to John Mitchell IV, funeral director and representative of the National Funeral Director Association, for his contributions and conversation.

I am very grateful to Dr. Kathy Armistead, my editor at Abingdon, for giving me the opportunity to write this book and for guidance and support along the way.

Though this book is about dying, I offer my undying love to Warren, my beloved husband, in this life and in life eternal.

Introduction

Death happens. Often it happens at the most inopportune times—for the deceased, for the family, and, to be honest, for us as pastors. We might receive a phone call or a text: "You're needed right away." Whatever else we had planned takes a backseat. We go—to the hospice house, the funeral home, the trauma center, the nursing home, the hospital room, or to the family home. We go into the unknown. Even if we've long been walking with the family through the valley of the shadow, death can bring surprise. When we're less familiar with the situation, there are more unknowns. As we approach the scene, we have questions: *Has dying been painful? Who will be present? Will emotions be out of control? Where is God for these folks?* We're thinking: *What will I say? When can I meet with the family? How am I going to have time to prepare a funeral? When can we schedule the funeral?* When entering the realm of the dying or the just-deceased, we never know for certain what awaits. Death and funerals are complex.

Our arrival is met with a mixture of responses. Some want a sign of God's presence when God seems absent or powerless. Others worry about how much religiosity we will bring. Others want this over and done with. Still others haven't been in the presence of death before and don't know what to expect. Confused, they want clarity regarding next steps. All eyes are on the pastor. No pressure.

I remember being summoned to a death scene. I arrived at the trauma center to see a twenty-two-year-old who had fallen thirty feet, had hit his head, and wasn't expected to live. As I entered the trauma bay, I tried not to look at his leg—the shiny whiteness jutting out from raw, red, mangled muscle. *That's bone,* I remember thinking. As I approached the patient, the doctor began to adjust his leg, saying, "This is going to hurt." The young man let out a piercing, guttural scream. I turned to leave. Then I stopped cold and asked, *Where am I going? I have a role here: this is my work.* As pastor, I—we—are called to places of pain, of dying, of death. We're called to stand alongside the screaming—whether of the dying or the grieving—and somehow to help to make sense or meaning of it all even when we, ourselves, are screaming on the inside. The young man died within the day. I was with the doctor when he gave the news to the devastated parents. I stayed with them as they cried, held each other, called relatives, and went to see and pray with their son's broken body. "I wouldn't want your job," the trauma doctor later told me, "It's too hard."

Death is hard, and it is the result of a process that happens over time. Likewise a funeral is not a one-time event but is part of the family and friends' grieving process. And, as we know, ministering through the funeral, though challenging, is one of the great privileges in ministry. Though we can never completely be prepared for death, and though funeral planning is never easy, there are particular approaches and perspectives that are appropriate through the funeral process. This book offers ways to be prepared and ways to name and separate various (and often contradicting) needs, while re-presenting the deceased as a child of God and being faithful to the deceased, to the grieving, to God, and to ourselves. In short, this guide assists the pastor in providing a ministry of presence and hope before, during, and after the funeral.

Throughout this guide, I use the image of "funeral story." I use this image to draw attention to both the content and the flow of the process of care. The guiding philosophy of the story approach to funeral planning is that there are many stories or perspectives surrounding each death. The framing thesis for this "how-to" book is that a hope-bringing funeral story is created in the intersections of five stories: stories of the deceased, the grieving family, the pastor, and the congregation or assembled grievers, and God's unfolding story of loving presence and future hope.

The story image also has to do with flow. The funeral process has a beginning, a middle, and an end: Preparing for Death (chapter 1), Caring through Anticipated Death (chapter 2), Caring through Sudden Death (chapter 3), Meeting with Family before the Funeral Service (chapter 4), Creating the Funeral Service (chapter 5), Creating the Funeral Sermon (chapter 6), and Following Up with Grievers (chapter 7).

In chapter one, "Preparing for Death," the book introduces a story-centered approach to the funeral process, by discussing each of the five stories, including how we can understand God's story in relation to death and grieving. Then the chapter elaborates on the stories of the dying or deceased and the grievers, the pastor's own story, and the congregation's story.

Chapter two, "Caring through Anticipated Death," elaborates on aspects of caring for the dying and grieving in situations concerning long-term illness or condition. Being attentive to the five intersecting stories, there are nine key principles the pastor can employ in this phase of the funeral process.

Then chapter three, "Caring through Sudden Death," discusses particular challenges involved in sudden-death situations, offering an A-B-C model for framing pastoral intervention as pastors attend to the intersections of the five stories at this phase of the funeral process.

In chapter four, "Meeting with Family before the Funeral Service," there are ways that the pastor can assist the family in five "tasks of grieving," while also gaining insights and information to be used in creating the funeral service and sermon. Here you will also find a discussion of three functions of funerals, particularly the ways in which these three functions are achieved through the intersections of the five stories of the deceased, grievers, congregation, pastor, and God.

Chapter five, "Creating the Funeral Service," discusses the creation of a meaningful funeral service that carries out the functions of the funeral described in chapter four. Here you will find a variety of funeral services, offering examples of ways to incorporate the intersections of the five stories into various components of the funeral service.

In chapter six, "Creating the Funeral Sermon," you will find a description of the functions of funeral sermons and examples of sermons that carry out these functions through the integration of stories.

Chapter seven, "Following Up with Grievers," outlines some understandings about grief that are emerging from recent research. The chapter elaborates on five pastoral practices that the pastor can use in following up with grievers after the funeral service. And finally, the appendix includes various templates to assist with the funeral process.

Throughout this book, you will find various scenarios, vignettes, sermons, and service examples. Although these draw on real situations, the examples are composites. In all cases, the names and details have been significantly changed.

Death is not easy. Walking through the valley of the shadow with others requires pastoral skills and strategies. This guide will help us, as pastors, give the grieving a lasting gift of God's loving presence and hope.

Chapter 1

Preparing for Death

Funerals take place in the context of life. We pastors know this to be true. In the midst of our sermon preparation, committee meetings, and pastoral visits, we receive the call or the text that someone is facing imminent death or has died. Everyday life is interrupted by death. We immediately rearrange pastoral and personal obligations to begin the funeral process. What sort of process will that be? Will it be simply a series of tasks—first visit with the family, then contact the funeral home, and then prepare a funeral message? Or will we connect our various acts of ministry and integrate our stories of grief with God's stories of loving presence and hope? This book takes the second view and will help you offer a significant and lasting gift to those who grieve for the deceased. Accordingly, the book looks at the funeral as a process that involves five sets of participants whose stories intersect throughout. These five stories include those of the dying or deceased, the loved ones—or "grievers"—the congregation, the pastor, and God.

Our central task as pastors through the funeral process is to recognize and facilitate the intersections among these stories. By weaving together these stories and by locating them in the context of God's story of loving presence and future hope, the funeral process can help grievers make meaning of this death and of their ongoing life story that has been interrupted by death.

This chapter comprises six sections. Section 1 introduces and justifies a story-centered approach to the funeral process; section 2 elaborates on how we can understand God's story in relation to death and grieving; section 3 tells the stories of the dying or deceased and of grieving people (section 4) before focusing on the pastor's own story and preparation for dealing with death and funerals (section 5). In the final section, there is the story of the congregation, including ways that the pastor can prepare the congregation for the inevitability of death (section 6).

Death is never easy. Scripture says that death is the enemy (1 Corinthians 15:26), yet death is a very natural part of our finite being. Death ends a person's life story, yet it touches the living stories of countless others. The pastor, by artfully weaving together the stories of the deceased, the grievers, the congregation, and the pastor and by locating all in the context of God's unfolding story, manifests God's loving presence and future hope.

1. A Story-centered Approach

A life story comprises events that are linked together to form a plotline. This plotline involves characters, relationships, and interactions, including conflict and resolution. A life story has a setting—the particular time and place, familial and societal contexts that provide structure and values in which we participate or ignore or resist to varying degrees. And a life story has recurring perspectives and points of view, values, and worldview by which we connect and interpret experiences, making meaning of various events. These perspectives, points of view, value, and worldview are how we make sense of things or how we make meaning of our lives.

We make meaning in relation to various factors, but as Christian people, we have the opportunity to make meaning of life and death in terms of our understanding of God. The ways in which we understand God working in the world and in our lives affect the ways that we interpret events. For instance, if Mary's cancer returns even after months of prayer for continued remission, Mary may interpret the illness as God's punishment. Mary has made meaning according to her understanding of a punitive God who has always judged her. However, Meg may feel God's loving presence in the midst of her illness. She interprets her illness as another opportunity to receive God's comfort. The ways that we make meaning in our life stories affect how we respond to our circumstances.

Pastors are also in the business of meaning making. Eugene Peterson, in looking back at his fifty years in ministry, reflects that he has been "a pastor in a community of storymaking."[1] By "story," he means:

a way of language that insists that persons cannot be known by reducing them to what they do, how they perform, the way they look. Story uses a language in which listening has joint billing with speaking. Story is language put to the use of discovering patterns and meanings—beauty and truth and goodness: Father, Son, and Holy Spirit. In the seemingly random and disconnected pieces of experience and dreams, tasks and songs, promises and betrayals that make up daily life, words and sentences detect and reveal and fashion stories in places of hospitality.

Pastors live in the story-hearing, story-making, and Bible-story-telling world. Especially in times of illness and death, pastors help people interpret their stories in the context of God's story. But how? How does a pastor stand in that busy intersection of interrelated stories? First, understand them.

2. God's Story

Particularly appropriate to the funeral context are two important themes in the story of how God offers God's self to be with God's people. As pastors, through ministry, we want to demonstrate and model God's loving presence and future hope. These two overlapping themes are not meant to be comprehensive, nor do they diminish the mystery and majesty of God. But especially in times of death and grief, God's people particularly resonate with these two themes, either in their presence or in their perceived absence. Often, these two themes are found together in biblical passages, such as the twenty-third Psalm. This beautiful and powerful psalm proclaims God's reassuring presence in the midst of difficult circumstances: "Even though I walk through the darkest valley, I fear no evil; for you are with me; your rod and your staff—they comfort me" (Psalm 23:4). The psalm also proclaims future hope in these difficult circumstances: "I shall dwell in the house of the LORD my whole life long" (Psalm 23:6). It is no surprise that this passage is commonly used at both deathbeds and funerals. It is also no surprise that Psalm 23 immediately follows Psalm 22. As Psalm 23 offers God's ever-present protection, Psalm 22 is a lament that begins with complaints about God's absence: "My God, my God, why have you forsaken me? Why are you so far from helping me, from the words of my groaning? O my God, I cry by day, but you do not answer; and by night, but find no rest" (Psalm 22:1-2). Ironically, the psalmist accuses God of being absent from and forsaking him yet addresses the complaint to God, as though God were present in his "groaning." Presence and absence accompany each other. Like other lament psalms, Psalm 22 moves from this raw expression of emotion—in this case, feelings of abandonment—to the confident expression that, by the close of the Psalm,

God will be faithful to God's people and provide a hopeful future different from the forlorn present. The people will testify to God's redeeming actions that constitute this hopeful future: "Future generations will be told about the Lord, and proclaim his deliverance to a people yet unborn, saying that he has done it" (Psalm 22:30b-31). God's story is one of loving presence with and future hope for God's people even and especially in the experience of death and grieving. The pastor represents God's story of loving presence and future hope throughout the funeral process.

God's gracious presence suffers with and comforts dying and grieving people. But some also experience the "shadow side" including God's perceived absence, judgment, indifference, and punishment. And in speaking of future hope, as pastors, we embrace both the specific resurrection hope in Jesus Christ and the general hope of a new, different, and life-giving future in God's purposes for grieving people in their unfolding next chapters. These two themes of loving presence and future hope are significant for the story of how God is with God's people in times of dying and grief, a story the pastor represents throughout.

Phil and Barbara tithed, worshiped in church every Sunday, raised their children in the church, sang in the choir, and served on committees. When Amy, their thirteen-year-old daughter, developed leukemia, church members held prayer vigils and sent cards, flowers, and casseroles. When Amy died, Phil and Barbara felt abandoned by God. They could not understand or make meaning of this tragic, senseless ending to their daughter's life story that was so full of promise. Phil and Barbara were angry at and disappointed in God, whom they saw as either powerless or merciless to save their daughter.

Phil and Barbara's pastor accompanied them through their valley of the shadow of grief. She was an agent and representative of God's love, manifesting both through her compassionate presence. She heard their anger against God, recognizing that their stories were intersecting with God's story in the tradition of lament. The pastor, feeling no need to defend God, committed to accompanying the couple through the devastation of their grief as they attempted to make meaning of Amy's death and of their life stories after this tragedy. As appropriate, and as the couple could hear them, the pastor spoke words of God's loving presence with and care for Amy and for them. Members of the congregation "companioned" them. Eventually, the couple was able to make meaning of Amy's death by adding a new and different chapter to their life stories. They made meaning by giving up the need to understand how God could have allowed this. Very slowly, the experience of being abandoned by God merged into a sense of God's suffering and loving presence with them. They were eventually able to accept the paradox that Amy had died and that this loving God suffered with them. Though they still grieve and miss Amy every day, they found meaning in their ongoing lives by volunteering at a children's hospital and helping other parents who were dealing with their children's diseases. Through working with other parents and experiencing God's grace in new ways, they were able to live into a hopeful future. The pastor's ongoing representation of God's loving presence and future hope helped Barbara and Phil make it through the valley of their grief.

As the pastor's presence with Barbara and Phil indicates, these themes of God's loving, hopeful presence exemplify a way that pastors can represent and manifest God's story when accompanying others through the valley of the shadow of death. We can observe three ways in which the pastor embodied God's story. First, she attuned herself to their needs. She was present and nonjudgmental. She did not defend God. She did not rebuke their protests to God. She did not attempt to "fix" them with platitudes. She held and cared for their stories as they unfolded. People grieve in different ways. Some want prayers, anointing, or to receive Communion. Some appreciate a gentle hand on the shoulder and silent, comforting presence. The point is that the pastor be attuned and responsive to particular people in ways particular to them.

Second, a pastor offers consistency of care and consistency of message. Death is a scary time. The dying and loved ones are facing the unknown, and this can involve much anxiety and uncertainty, even among the faithful. Fear and faith are not mutually exclusive. Phil and Barbara feel angry and abandoned by God. Greta worries about what will happen to her divorcing daughter and grandchildren after she dies. Joe doesn't know how he'll survive the death of his wife of fifteen years. These losses and unknown futures provoke fear and anxiety that can be lessened by the presence of a trusted companion, who is a secure base of comfort and care. No matter what the circumstance, the pastor represents God in Christ, who is the ultimate source of comfort and care to these grieving people. Through consistency of care that demonstrates a message of God's love, the pastor helps the dying and the grieving know that God is present with them in their suffering. And subsequently, as they make meaning of the death through ongoing grief work, the pastor helps in the construction of a more hopeful future.

Third, the pastor includes the congregation in providing consistency of care and consistency of the message of God's love. Throughout the funeral process, the congregation can manifest God's love and care through acts of presence and kindness. Section 6 returns to specific ways the congregation

5

can provide consistency of care and message throughout the funeral process. The pastor, then, represents and embodies God's story of loving presence and future hope as God's story intersects with each of the other stories.

3. Stories of the Dying or Deceased

In addition to God's story, the second of the five intersecting stories concerns the dying or deceased. A funeral story always assumes a death story. Death stories come in different forms—some imminent, some sudden. A nursing-home resident is in her last days. A teenager is killed by a drunk driver. A baby is stillborn. A woman who had Alzheimer's disease for nine years dies in her sleep. A sixty-two-year-old woman collapses in the garage with a heart attack.

Everyone involved in the death sees the dying or deceased differently. Doctors and nurses see the person as a patient manifesting a particular disease or condition. Loved ones view the deceased in terms of a relationship and life story forever changed. The pastor, in intersecting the dying or deceased with God's story, sees and represents the person in her or his truest identity—as a child of God.

Throughout the funeral process, the pastor functions to present again or re-present the deceased as a child of God who is embraced in God's love and is returning to God's eternal, loving presence. The pastor demonstrates this perspective through consistency of care (by being present to the dying and deceased person) and consistency of message (that God is present with this person through life, through death, and beyond death). The pastor offers assurance that nothing, not even death, separates the dying or deceased from God's love: "For I am convinced that neither death, nor life, nor angels, nor rulers, nor things present, nor things to come, nor powers, nor height, nor depth, nor anything else in all creation, will be able to separate us from the love of God in Christ Jesus our Lord" (Romans 8:38-39).

In re-presenting the person's life and death story in the context of God's story, the pastor assists the dying person in making meaning of his or her life and death as a child of God. By being present with the dying/deceased throughout the dying process and attending to spiritual needs, the pastor affirms not only that this person's death and life matter but also that this person is a beloved child of God. This life and death are embraced within the context of God's larger story, which the pastor represents.

Throughout the funeral process, the pastor re-presents the deceased as a child of God who is embraced in God's love and is returning to God's eternal presence. The pastor recognizes and re-presents this person's identity as one who was created in the image of God, was formed by God in his or her mother's womb, and had a life story with a beginning and an end, a life story that is in the context of God's gracious story. Throughout the funeral process, the pastor honors and re-presents particular intersections of this person's life and death story with God's story and the stories of loved ones whom this life has touched.

4. Stories of the Grieving

The stories of God and of the deceased affect the stories of other people. When one person dies, a relationship in its present form dies as well. The third story in this intersection of stories includes those of grieving family and friends.

Each person's grief is experienced differently and individually, just as each individual and relationship with the deceased is different. Take, for example, the death of sixteen-year-old Toby, who is killed in a car crash by a young drunk driver. We have the parents' stories of devastating grief and anger. There is also the guilt-saturated story of the other driver who caused the crash. There's the devastating shame of the driver's parents (possibly also belonging to your church). There's the grief story of the younger sister who adored her big brother. There are the other youth-group kids who "can't understand how God could let this happen." Emotions are raw, diverse, and conflicted. By carefully and repeatedly hearing each of the different stories of grief without judgment and with compassion, the pastor shows consistency of care through a ministry of presence. By attending care-fully to these stories, the pastor also gains insights into ways in which to weave these stories of devastating grief, pain, and loss into a funeral narrative that cares for grievers while also re-presenting the deceased and proclaiming God's loving presence and future hope.

Though no two people grieve in the same way, research shows that there are commonalities in the tasks that grievers face in the grief process. The ways that grievers approach these tasks may be different, but the tasks remain the same. Especially in relation to the funeral process, there are five "tasks of grievers."[2]

    (1) to accept the reality of the death,
    (2) to express grief around the death,
    (3) to make meaning of the deceased's life and death,

(4) to adjust to a world in which the deceased is no longer physically present, and

(5) to redefine the relationship with the deceased in terms of memory, legacy, and love.

Addressing these tasks is crucial, and we will return to them regularly throughout this book.

Accepting the reality of the death has to do with acknowledging the ending of a life story. *Expressing grief around the death* involves expressing whatever emotions are appropriate for an individual. For some, this may mean tearfully telling a story over and over again. Others may retreat into silence. Some may feel profound sadness. Others may feel relief, pride, or gratitude when thinking about the deceased. Still others may want to celebrate the deceased's life. *Making meaning of the deceased's life and death* is the central task of grief work, as discussed above. Also included in this task is making meaning of the griever's life story now that this death has interrupted the narrative. *Adjusting to a world where the deceased is no longer physically present* involves adapting to physical, social, relational, and functional changes that the death precipitates. The ways in which a griever adjusts to a life without the deceased will vary, depending on the kind of relationship the griever had with the deceased. The lack of the deceased's physical presence does not mean the relationship has to end. *Redefining the relationship with the deceased in terms of memory, legacy, and love* recognizes an ongoing relationship.

Research indicates that it is healthy for those who want to continue to have emotional attachments to deceased loved ones to continue to do so (see chapter 7). "Continuing bonds" can occur by recalling fond memories. Connection can be maintained by carrying out a legacy left behind by the deceased. For instance, if a baby died of Sudden Infant Death Syndrome (SIDS), parents may feel connected to their baby by contributing to SIDS research. If a grandmother loved quilting, her daughter and granddaughters may meet monthly for a period of time to quilt and tell stories about Grandma. Another way to stay connected is through feelings of love and closeness. Barbara kept Amy's room the way she left it. From time to time, she'd sit at Amy's desk, surrounded by her things, and feel love for and closeness with her daughter.

Although it is important that grievers accomplish all of these five tasks, these tasks are not linear. Grievers do not necessarily move through the tasks in any orderly fashion, predictable timetable, or predetermined sequence. This again demonstrates the individuality of a griever's process in that each task is addressed in a griever's own time. The "task model" is helpful to pastors, however, as it offers a way to assess issues with which a griever is struggling and to offer appropriate interventions around a specific task.

As the pastor accompanies grievers through their grief, it is necessary to be aware of the pastor's own story around grief and loss.

5. The Pastor's Story

Part of the pastor's story concerns the pastor's role as a representative of God's loving presence and future hope. As noted in section 2, the pastor represents God's story by being attuned and responsive to a griever's particular needs, by offering consistency of care and message, and by involving members of the congregation as appropriate.

The other important aspect of the pastor's story concerns our own experiences of and beliefs around death. Each of us brings our own dying, death, and loss stories to every death experience. Our story may be that we don't like hospitals and that we are squeamish at the sight of blood.

Perhaps we are relatively young and have not experienced significant loss. We may feel ill equipped to minister to those experiencing devastating loss. Or we may have experienced profound or recent loss that causes us to want to distance ourselves from death or to interpret the death through our own unprocessed grief and loss. Or we may have experienced many deaths and funerals and therefore bring a "professional" bearing that trades in stereotypes rather than the specific nuances of each situation. We may fear that we are too emotional or not emotional enough. Our story may be that we are too busy or overwhelmed in the day-to-day life of church to attend patiently to what can feel like the all-consuming needs of the grieving who just should "get a life."

Whatever our story, it intersects with the stories of others in the funeral process. Therefore, it is important to come to grips with our own death experiences or lack thereof and how we cope or haven't coped with them. If we deny our own wounds and grief, for example, we risk the danger of projecting our hurts and our own self-solutions onto others. If we have not worked through our own grief stories sufficiently, we may allow ourselves to become overly involved and to overly identify with the pain in a way that incapacitates us. Or we may insulate ourselves emotionally to the extent that we are not fully present to grievers. By getting in touch with our own stories of loss, we can be better companions to others in their grief.

Here are some suggestions to help.

- Do a "Loss Graph" of all losses. Draw a horizontal timeline and date every significant loss you have experienced. Include loss of pets, loss of romantic relationships, financial loss, loss of security, and physical deaths. Allow yourself to feel the loss of each event. About each loss, ask, *is there anything I need to forgive or ask forgiveness for? Are there other words about this relationship or this loss that have been left unsaid?* It can be helpful to write these statements in a journal or letterform, even if we do not send the letter.

- Be attentive to grief and loss in the congregation. Be a student of grief. Pay attention to seasonal rhythms of life and death and rebirth. Gather songs and poems and stories in a file to help remind you of how deeply inspiring death can be. People are often grateful to have the opportunity to share their grief. By listening carefully, we have the opportunity to learn the myriad ways that grief affects people.

- If you have experienced recent or profound loss, grieve the loss. Listen to music, journal, pray, read Scripture, look at photos, be silent, cry—whatever helps to feel and process the emotions.

- Engage Henri Nouwen's "wounded healer"[3] approach to ministry. Nouwen names the importance of pastors looking after and healing our own wounds in order to be able to help heal the wounds of others. Also read Nouwen's *Our Greatest Gift*[4] and Thomas Lynch's *Undertaking: Life Studies from the Dismal Trade.*[5]

- To better acquaint yourself with hospital visitation and emergencies, call the pastoral care department or the chaplain of the local hospital. Ask to shadow a chaplain during visitation rounds and on trauma calls so as to be exposed to situations of sickness and death.

- Ask to visit the ICU, neonatal care, oncology, or any other areas of specialty so as to increase familiarity with the experiences of the sick and vulnerable.

- Establish relationships with funeral home directors—especially ones whom church folk often use for funerals. Ask to shadow them throughout their process from when they pick up a body to when it is ready for a funeral. Ask them what people expect them to provide and how you can help them. Ask them about their procedures and service guidelines.

• Sort out your own end-of-life care preferences and complete appropriate forms, such as a living will and a medical power of attorney.

• Consult with local hospice and bereavement counselors about grief.

• Have congregational systems of care in place that can help spread the responsibility and privilege of caring for the dying and grieving (see section 5). Pastors can feel overwhelmed with the challenge of expressing continual care for the dying and grieving. While the size of the congregation and the pastoral staff will influence the time a pastor is able to spend with a family, it's also important for the pastor to realize self-limits around "compassion fatigue" and the need for self-care.

Attention to one's personal issues around death and loss enables the pastor to become a better companion to the dying and grieving. Alan Wolfelt provides a helpful guide to "companioning" with grieving people (see the following page).[6] This companioning model is helpful for several reasons. First, it does not require the pastor to be an "expert" on grief. This model assumes that grievers are the experts in their own grief and that grievers will "teach" the pastor how to accompany them if the pastor is attentive. Second, this model affirms that when there has been significant loss, grieving takes time. When a pastor and a congregation become safe places for people to grieve, the mourning are able to be comforted (Matthew 5:4). Third, the companioning model allows for the presence of mystery. When the pastor enters the wilderness of another's grief with a heart that is open to the griever and to God, God's loving presence and future hope are manifest.

Fundamental to this approach is how the pastor listens to grievers' stories. Especially in times of grief, it is important that pastors do not listen to life-and-death stories with judgment or with any agenda. Set aside plenty of time to listen. It is important that pastors do not listen to stories to solve, fix, or "treat" the grief. Rather, the pastor's role is to walk alongside grievers and to help bear their particular burdens. By walking alongside and companioning grievers through the valley of the shadow of death, a pastor's presence represents God's loving presence and future hope. At the same time, be attuned to the possibility that some grief is more complicated than others and some people may need other types of professional help in the long-term.

Alan Wolfelt's Model of Companioning the Bereaved

- Companioning is about being present to another person's pain; it is not about taking away the pain.
- Companioning is about going to the wilderness of the soul with another human being; it is not about thinking you are responsible for finding the way out.
- Companioning is about honoring the spirit; it is not about focusing on the intellect.
- Companioning is about listening with the heart; it is not about analyzing with the head.
- Companioning is about bearing witness to the struggles of others; it is not about judging or directing these struggles.
- Companioning is about walking alongside; it is not about leading or being led.
- Companioning means discovering the gifts of sacred silence; it does not mean filling up every moment with words.
- Companioning the bereaved is about being still; it is not about frantic movement forward.
- Companioning is about respecting disorder and confusion; it is not about imposing order and logic.
- Companioning is about learning from others; it is not about teaching them.
- Companioning is about curiosity; it is not about expertise.

The pastor's story, then, consists of two dimensions—our own experiences of loss and grief and the role of being an agent of God's loving presence and future hope. In order to accomplish the latter, we need to have done our own work with the former.

6. Stories of the Congregation

In addition to the stories of God, the deceased, the grieving, and the pastor, congregational stories are also interwoven with the funeral process. By *congregation,* I refer to the members and regular attendees of the pastor's church. For any given funeral, a particular group of grievers forms that may overlap considerably with the congregation or may have a very tangential relationship to it, with degrees in between. To distinguish between the two, I use the term *congregation* to refer to the church body. I use the phrase *assembled grievers* to refer to the community that gathers for a particular funeral.

The congregation is continuously composing a story around death. Death may be at the foreground of the congregational story if there has been a recent, sudden, tragic death or if some members have recently died or if the congregation as a whole is aged. However, if the congregation is largely composed of younger people, death may be a more distant story. Or, the story of death in our congregation may be a silent story, in that we often don't discuss death other than at funerals. Or, the story may be that we speak of death, but only in terms of "life celebration," because we think that to allow and even encourage open acknowledgments of death and expressions of grief somehow demonstrates a lack of faith and undermines the "victory over the last enemy."

Various understandings about death emerge around funerals. Some or all of these understandings might be expressed:

- Death is the enemy, often implying that the deceased has lost the battle.
- God has won the victory over death.
- The pain, suffering, and tragedy of the death obliterate the person's life story.
- Death is an opportunity to celebrate life.
- Death is a pathway to sainthood; one speaks no evil about the dead.
- Death releases the soul to be with God.
- Death awaits the resurrection of the body.
- Death is an entrance to heaven where all loved ones will be reunited with one another and with God.
- Death is an opportunity for God's tender grace and care for grievers.

13

- Death is an opportunity to continue the life of the deceased through memories and legacy.
- Death is the ultimate end with no afterlife to come.

Pastors not only listen to stories about death in the congregation. We also have the opportunity to shape these understandings. Adult education classes, sermons, and care programs such as Stephen Ministry offer theological, pastoral, and pragmatic perspectives on and support for death and dying.

Listed below are suggestions as to ways that pastors can prepare congregations for death.

- Offer an adult-education or a small-group series on grief and death. Invite guest speakers from the congregation and community to talk about death, dying, and grieving. Appropriate personnel might include:
    - o Hospice chaplains;
    - o Medical ethics experts who address the kind of medical ethical decisions people face at death;
    - o Hospital chaplains to offer perspectives around a "good death";
    - o Grief counselors;
    - o Medical workers from trauma and ICU who might offer preventative advice;
    - o Legal professionals who discuss living wills, last will and testaments, advance directives, and medical powers of attorney.
- Encourage the congregation to formalize end-of-life preferences through an advance directive, which is a legal document that allows a person to convey preferences for end-of-life care. It also provides for a proxy decision-maker to be identified should the person no longer be able to make decisions. Each state has its own laws for creating advance directives. It is helpful if the pastor is familiar with his or her own state law.
- *The Living Pulpit* elaborates on one example of a curriculum around death: see Ginger Brab and Judith Hoch Wray, "Leaders Guide for Adult Education, from Text to Life: Death" (July-September 1998). They suggest topics for a nine-session series for which they provide resources and outlines.

1. Introduction to Death
2. Theologies of Death (1 Corinthians 15:12-58)
3. Death, Baptisms, and Eucharist (Romans 5:1-11; 1 Corinthians 1:18-25)
4. Thoughts on Immortality; Reading or Summarizing Such Theologians as Paul Tillich and Jürgen Moltmann.
5. Death and the Meaning of Life; How Death Helps Us to Reevaluate Life
6. Life, Death, and Justice
7. Controversial Death Issues (The Death Penalty and Euthanasia)
8. Caring for the Dying
9. Loss and Mourning

- PBS offers a comprehensive series on dying called *On Our Own Terms: Moyers on Dying,* complete with leader and discussion guide (www.pbs.org/onourownterms). It covers topics such as: making plans for the end of life, what doctors want to know from their patients, managing pain, and further steps you can take with your family and in your community.

- Establish a Stephen Ministry or other congregational care program that trains parishioners to care for the dying and grieving. See *The Caring Congregation: How to Become One and Why It Matters* by Karen Lampe (Nashville: Abingdon Press, 2011).

- In his book *Getting through Grief: Caregiving by Congregations* (Nashville: Abingdon Press, 1993), Ronald Sunderland develops congregationally based ministries to the grieving. The book covers (1) Understanding Grief; (2) Working Through Grief; (3) Grief: Our Constant Companion; (4) Developing a Grief Ministry; (5) Grief Support: A Continuing Ministry; and (6) Grief Education.

- For a practical and comprehensive grief kit, see Harold Ivan Smith's *The Grief Care Kit: Bereavement Resources for Counselors and Recovery Group Leaders* (Kansas City, MO: Beacon Hill Press, 2008). This includes a one-hour DVD called "Ministering in Times of Loss," complete resources for establishing mutual-care grief groups, and useful templates for pastors as they reach out to grieving people.

- Practical and useful is Howard Stone's *The Caring Church: A Guide for Lay Pastoral Care* (Minneapolis: Augsburg Press, 1991). Topics include the care relationship, listening and responding, hospital and shut-in visitation, caregiving to grievers, and special situations.

- Set up groups to prepare funeral dinners for grieving families and friends after funerals. Trained volunteers understand this to be an active ministry with grieving people that goes beyond the kitchen to caring and informed personal interactions.

- Preach about suffering, death, and grieving. The *Revised Common Lectionary* provides ample opportunities to name God's loving presence and future hope, including the resurrection hope of Christ. Be attentive to the scheduling of lament psalms and especially to the portions of despair and grief that the lectionary selections often omit.

- Have some books on hand or in the church library such as these: *When the One You Love Is Gone* by Rebekah L. Miles (Nashville: Abingdon Press, 2012) and *Healing the Heartbreak of Grief* by Peter James Flamming (Nashville: Abingdon Press, 2010).

The pastor who thoughtfully prepares the congregation to face their own deaths, the deaths of their loved ones, and the deaths of church members does a great service to the congregation. Those who encounter death and grief will then be better prepared to experience the living presence of God through the living presence of the community that walks with them through the valley of the shadow. When twenty-five-year-old Eric Wolterstorff died in a mountaineering accident, his father, Nicholas, said that at the funeral, the church community's symbols and actions spoke as much as the words. The gathered people celebrated the Eucharist, "that sacrament of God's participation in our brokenness." They "came forward successively in groups, standing in circles around the coffin, passing the signs of Christ's brokenness to each other." The funeral did not take away the loss of Eric. But it did do something else, Wolterstorff writes. "It sank deep into me the realization that my son's death is not all there is."[7]

Death is not the end of the story. God promises that life and love triumph over death and that hope triumphs over despair. The congregation has a role in bringing this hope to life.

16

Conclusion

This chapter described the five stories that intersect throughout the funeral process as the pastor creates a cohesive and connected funeral story: God's story and the stories of the deceased, the grieving, the pastor, and the congregation. In the next chapter, we will focus on these stories in relation to one type of death—that of anticipated death.

Chapter 2

Caring through Anticipated Death

Death happens in all sorts of ways. For the purposes of our discussion of the pastor's roles throughout the funeral process, we'll look at death according to two broad categories. The first category is anticipated death after a long-term illness or condition. The second category (see chapter 3) is sudden death after a brief illness, accident, or suicide. Each kind of death creates the possibilities for various appropriate pastoral interventions, which are part of the funeral process.

This chapter begins with a story of a long-term illness of a parishioner (section 1). Then in section 2, emerging from this case study, there are nine key principles for the funeral process, which is underway long before death takes place. Throughout, we are attentive to the five stories of the dying person, the grievers, the congregation, the pastor, and God.

Betty's Story

Before breaking her hip, Betty, an eighty-two-year-old parishioner, was an active church member. She attended worship regularly, taught an adult Sunday school class, and served on various committees. A widow for ten years, she lived alone and enjoyed her autonomy. When she broke her hip and went into a convalescent care facility, her health began declining. She came down with pneumonia and showed increasing signs of dementia, which her doctor attributed to a series of strokes. As Betty's hip healed, medical personnel encouraged Betty either to seek out an assisted living facility or to live with family with assistance from home health care.

Betty's pastor had been regularly visiting her at the convalescent care center. Betty told him that she really wanted to return to her home but that her doctors said she shouldn't live alone. Betty said that she missed her home filled with memories of Walter, her deceased husband, and of their two grown children, Pam and Ben. She missed her garden. And Betty valued her independence and didn't want "to be a burden on anyone."

Betty's daughter, Pam, was also a member of the congregation. Faced with a decision regarding Betty's care, Pam met with her pastor. She explained the situation, saying that she wanted her mother to live with her family, but her husband, Bob, an inactive church member, objected, saying that they didn't have the time or resources to care responsibly for Betty, given their small home, jobs, and two daughters' busy high-school lives. Pam said her younger brother, Ben, not a church member, was divorced, was struggling financially, and did not have the means to take care of Betty in his apartment. Ben wanted their mother to go to an assisted living facility. Pam named her resentment toward her husband and brother for their "callous disregard for my mom." The social worker at the convalescent center had suggested a family conference. Pam requested that the pastor attend this meeting. He agreed. He also checked in with Betty. Later, he met with Pam and Bob's daughters, who were concerned about both their grandma and mom.

During the meeting, both the pastor and the social worker diligently ensured that all perspectives were shared, including those of medical personnel and all family members. Betty shared her sadness about the possibility of moving into the facility but also her desire not to be a burden on her family. Pam expressed her preference for her mother to move in with her family and said that she would leave her job to take care of her mother. Bob said, "You know we can't afford for you to leave your job." Betty started to cry and said she didn't want to be a burden. Ben said, "Mom, you'll get the best care at Prairie Oaks. And you'll make friends who can keep you company." Bob said, "We only want what's best for your health." Pam fumed as her husband and brother spoke. Pam cried at the end of the meeting when Betty announced that she had decided to move to the facility. Bob and Ben approved this decision. Pam did not, and there were strained relationships among the three of them. The pastor ended with prayer, naming the difficulty of this decision and asking God's presence with each person as they navigated this transition.

Betty moved into Prairie Oaks. The pastor continued to meet with family members. Betty and Pam separately discussed the emotional fallout with the pastor. Though Betty made the decision to go to the facility, she told the pastor that she felt she had no option and that she was "put here to die." Pam shared her continuing anger and resentment toward her husband and brother. To the pastor's surprise, Bob met with the pastor, admitting his strained relationship with an increasingly cold and hostile Pam. Bob also reported that Ben was feeling guilty that his divorce and financial situation meant he could not offer financial support for his mother. The pastor checked in with Pam and Bob's daughters after youth group. They said that they knew they should visit their grandma more, but they found the nursing home depressing.

Knowing that the family members would benefit from talking with one another, the pastor encouraged another family conference. Family members reluctantly agreed, requesting the pastor's presence. In the gathering, the pastor's leading questions about how they were coping allowed for honest expression of difficult emotions. Pam, Bob, and Ben each expressed their own feelings of guilt, regret, and sorrow. Betty seemed genuinely surprised at these feelings. She said she felt "terrible that everyone was feeling bad on my account." She admitted the difficulty of her transition, but she also said, "Honestly, this is the best place for me. I'm adjusting, and I don't want any of you to feel bad." She saw the tension among Pam, Bob, and Ben and strongly urged them to be at peace with one another. She also told her granddaughters not to feel guilty about not visiting, that she knew they had busy lives. Both granddaughters cried and hugged their grandma. At the end of the meeting, the emotional air seemed clearer. Bob, Ben, and the granddaughters assured Betty they would visit more often.

In subsequent months, the pastor continued to meet with Betty. With Betty's permission, he enlisted the congregational care system that involved trained church volunteers who also regularly visited her. The pastor found that increasingly Betty was reflecting on her memories. Over several visits, the pastor assisted her in a life review. Responding to his questions and prompts, Betty expressed her pride in her family and in her role in the church. She named her greatest pain—the stillbirth of her first child. The pastor had not known of this loss and listened carefully as Betty shared her pain and her hope to see her baby in heaven. She also shared her joy in being wife, mother, and faithful Christian. Overall, she said she thought God would say to her, "Well done, good and faithful servant."

As Betty's health declined over time, she openly talked about death—her fears, hopes, and preferences. The pastor asked, "What would a good death look like for you?" The pastor helped Betty complete an advance directive, in which she expressed her preference not to be kept alive by extraordinary measures if in a terminal condition. She talked about her preference to be buried next to Walter, where she would feel his closeness. Additionally, she shared ways that she felt God's loving presence, such as through her favorite hymns such as "Amazing Grace" and "I'll Fly Away" and through Scripture such as her favorite, the twenty-third Psalm. In her failing health, she said she felt like she was living the Footprints poem, in that God was carrying her. On subsequent visits, the pastor played these hymns from his iPhone and read her Psalm 23 and the Footprints poem.

On another occasion, the pastor asked Betty what she would miss when she died. She expressed regret that she probably would not be able to attend the weddings of her grandchildren. The pastor asked if she would want to write a letter or make a video or voice recording. Betty loved the idea of writing letters, which she did for both of her granddaughters. Both have a letter from their Grandma Betty, to be opened on their wedding days.

On one occasion when the family was visiting Betty, the pastor asked them what they would all miss about their life together. Among other memories, Betty, Pam, and the granddaughters shared the family tradition of making hard candy and cookies together at the holidays. Subsequently, Pam brought in her mother's recipe box, and together they identified significant recipes, most important the recipe for the candies that they made every Christmas. They were going to make a family recipe book.

Shortly after, Betty had a stroke and was taken to the hospital where she was in a coma and on life support. As Pam, Bob, Ben, and the granddaughters sat with Betty in her hospital room, they were warm and tender toward one another. The pastor played "I'll Fly Away" and "Amazing Grace" on his iPhone. During "Amazing Grace," the family circled Betty's bed and sang along.

The next day, the pastor joined the family in a meeting with the medical personnel. The doctor indicated that Betty showed no signs of brain activity. They referred to her advance directive, which indicated her preference not to be kept alive on life support. All agreed to remove life support, knowing it was Betty's wish. The pastor encouraged family members to express whatever they wanted to say to Betty. He respected their needs for privacy and left the room. He then gathered the family at her bed. They held hands as he read the twenty-third Psalm and the Footprints poem. He asked the family for their prayer requests. They wanted prayers for a peaceful, painless death for Betty and for strength for the family. The pastor incorporated these requests into his prayer. They prayed the Lord's Prayer together. Shortly after, the monitor indicated that Betty had died. Pam cried and hugged Bob, Ben, and her daughters. The family seemed at peace with one another and with Betty's death. The pastor realized that Betty had died "a good death" as she had hoped—surrounded by her family.

The nurse expressed sympathy and asked about funeral arrangements. The pastor watched as Ben shared his mother's preferences for a funeral home. The pastor reflected on the change in Ben over the last months as he had felt less guilty and more empowered to participate in his mother's care. The pastor asked the nurse how long the family could stay with Betty, and she said there was no rush. The pastor stayed with the family as they again circled Betty's body, touching her, kissing her forehead. The pastor let the family take the lead in doing what they needed to do to honor Betty's death. After a time of silence, they started sharing family stories. Laughter and tears were shared in this time of storytelling. The pastor, noting the significance of the holy and tender moments after death, made a note to remember these stories for funeral preparation. After a while, the family seemed ready to go.

The pastor walked the family to the parking lot. They arranged a time to meet the next day to talk about the funeral. The pastor drove home, feeling grateful for the long journey toward death that he had shared with Betty and her family. He realized that the journey would continue in their ongoing grief work and funeral service preparations.

Pastoral Interventions

From this scenario, we can observe nine key principles for effective pastoral care in the funeral process when it involves anticipated death after long-term illness or condition: (1) *respect and honor the sacred process of dying and death;* (2) *recognize that the funeral process begins before death;* (3) *take the office of pastor seriously;* (4) *attend to family systems;* (5) *help the dying person and the family prepare for death;* (6) *involve the congregation in care;* (7) *facilitate anticipatory grieving;* (8) *be prepared to be a liaison among the dying person, family, and medical personnel;* and (9) *be attentive to intersections with God's story.*

1. Respect and Honor the Sacred Process of Dying and Death

- Throughout Betty's story, the pastor honors her dignity, caring respectfully for her and her family. He understands her to be created in the image of God and interacts with her as a child of God. His actions are consistent with what has come to be known as a "dying person's bill of rights."[1]

Dying Person's Bill of Rights

o I have the right to be treated as a living human until I die.

o I have the right to maintain a sense of hopefulness, however changing its focus may be.

o I have the right to be cared for by those who can maintain a sense of hopefulness, however changing this may be.

o I have the right to express my feelings and emotions about my approaching death in my own way.

o I have the right to participate in decisions concerning my care.

o I have the right to expect continuing medical and nursing attention even though "cure" goals must be changed to "comfort" goals.

o I have the right not to die alone.

o I have the right to be free of pain.

o I have the right to have my questions answered honestly.

o I have the right to retain my individuality and not be judged for my decisions, which may be contrary to the belief of others.

o I have the right to expect that the sanctity of the human body will be respected after death.

o I have the right to be cared for by caring, sensitive, knowledgeable people who will attempt to understand my needs and will be able to gain some satisfaction in helping me face my death.

2. Recognize That the Funeral Process Begins before Death

- Even though Betty's death has not yet taken place, the pastor realizes that the funeral process has begun. Throughout, the pastor proactively facilitates a good death and healthy grieving.

- As Betty's situation declines and death seems to be more imminent, the pastor wisely attends to the various intersecting stories. He engages Betty, her daughter, Pam, and son, Ben, Pam's husband, and her granddaughters. Particularly, the pastor works with family to address conflicts over Betty's situation. The pastor is aware that unresolved issues complicate engaging the tasks of grieving after death occurs.

3. Take the Office of Pastor Seriously

- Being present with the dying and grieving requires a clear and empowering sense of one's pastoral identity and mission in the life of the folk. Pastors who are used to "doing" may not realize the healing effects of "being" with people throughout the process of transition, loss, and grief. By being present, the pastor represents God's loving presence and future hope. By being present and attuned to needs, the pastor enters the wilderness of another's loss and pain in the same way that Christ is present to us in all of our wildernesses.

- Accompanying people through the dying and funeral-preparation process can involve momentous decisions regarding end-of-life care, including withdrawal of life support, use of morphine, and whether or not to resuscitate. At these times of decisions come significant opportunities for pastoral care with lasting effects. The pastor can help the family name and face issues around death. Also, the pastor can use active and reflective listening in ways that help the dying and family members know their own preferences around decisions that need to be made.

- Taking initiative in dying and funeral contexts requires a deep level of care for parishioners and even those connected to the family who are not church members. The pastor reached out to all family members, even to Ben, who was not a member of the church.

4. Attend to Family Systems[2]

- The pastor realizes that Betty's life and death interacts with the stories of other family members as all attempt to make meaning of this death and its implications. Treat the crisis of the dying process as an opportunity to engage the entire relational system.

- The pastor optimizes the possibility of long-term healing by not anxiously rushing to apply short-term comfort measures that ignore difficult emotional and relational issues. Often, a pastor can feel pressure to bring comfort and peace. We can sense this pressure from family and medical staff, and we can put this pressure on ourselves. We know, though, that relationships are messy. There are no perfect families. Crisis can bring out the messiest in all of us. To do effective family systems work, we must fight the expectation and the belief that harmony, at the expense of honesty, is the way to comfort and peace. The pastor in Betty's story does not wave away her sense of being "put there to die." Nor does he minimize the relational difficulties of Pam, Bob, and Ben.

- The pastor realizes that family dynamics are exacerbated when family members are under stress, especially the stress that death brings. Pam has always been caretaker. Ben has always felt like the inadequate little brother. Bob has always been pragmatic. Betty has always been self-sacrificing. The intersection of these themes provokes inevitable conflict.

- The pastor encourages family members to talk to one another in addition to talking to the pastor. In private conversations, the pastor listens and helps family members name and understand their emotions as they struggle to make meaning of Betty's approaching death. The pastor encourages the family members to engage their differences and disagreements with one another directly.

- The pastor listens to all sides of the stories and tries not to take positions. The pastor realizes that it can be healing just to be heard. In the family conference and after, the pastor encourages honest and open expression of feelings.

- Not all families are so forthcoming. In many situations the pastor can help elicit and name key issues at stake for the dying person and family members. By asking insightful questions, the pastor helps surface deep fears. If, for example, the family meeting with Betty had been more contentious, the pastor could have asked Betty, hearing this conflict, "What is your biggest fear or concern right now?" She may have said something like, "I'm afraid that after I die, everyone will go on fighting." The pastor's encouragement to name a deep fear can change the conversation and the family dynamics. The truth is not easy, but the truth can set us free and help facilitate honest conversations before the fears materialize.

5. Help the Dying Person and the Family Prepare for Death

- As death becomes more imminent, the pastor is in a unique position to help the family system prepare for a "good death." A good death will vary depending on the person and the family circumstance. The best way to know what a good death means for these individuals is to ask with sensitivity and compassion and to listen carefully.

- It's helpful for the pastor to document or record key points from the conversation. Keep a file on all conversations that will be helpful for future funeral planning.

- The pastor facilitates the expression of end-of-life care preferences. The pastor helped Betty complete an advance directive so that her wishes and preferences for end-of-life care would be honored.

- The pastor helps the dying person do a life review. A life review is basically a sharing of stories that helps the dying person make meaning of his or her life. As the pastor thoughtfully and sensitively asks questions, the dying person might discover intersections between his or her story and God's story, or the pastor can name these intersections. Sample life review questions can include:

    o What in your life are you proud about?
    o Where was God in your proudest moments?
    o What are some of your disappointments?
    o Where was God in your disappointments?
    o What are your hopes for your family, friends, and church?
    o What would you like to see continue beyond your life?
    o What Bible story do you most relate to?
    o What are important scripture verses, stories, or parables that you would like your family to remember?
    o What are favorite hymns or songs and why?
    o How would you describe your family life?
    o How did your mother influence who you are?
    o How did your father influence who you are?
    o How did you meet your spouse?
    o What values did you instill in your children?
    o How would you like your family and friends to remember you?

o If God, in the person of Jesus, were sitting here in this chair, what would Jesus say about your life?

• If appropriate, the pastor might suggest activities for the dying person and family to do together. Options include writing a journal together; doing genealogy; organizing family photos, a scrapbook, or recipes as in Betty's story; planting a memory garden; putting together a collection of favorite things; and recording audio and video conversations. These activities can focus time together and create lasting memories.

• The pastor asks about the dying person's funeral preferences and encourages the person to share these preferences with family members.

• The pastor can also lead the dying person and loved ones in meaningful rituals. Rituals can help affirm the promise of God's loving presence mediated through memorable, symbolic actions. Rituals can include prayer. They can employ symbols, such as flowers or anointing of oil or laying on of hands. They can involve the hearing and reading of Scripture, poems, or other readings. They can involve Communion. They can include hymns and songs, perhaps played on a music player or phone or by family or church musicians.

• When death occurs, it is often beneficial for the pastor to accompany the family to the funeral home. A pastor's presence can be centering and grounding.

6. Involve the Congregation in Care

• In Betty's situation, the pastor uses a congregational care system set up for those in the process of dying. See chapter 1, section 5 for examples of care systems.

• The pastor or designated representative from such a care system can regularly ask the dying and the family, "What do you need right now?" and find resources from the congregation to meet these needs. Members of the congregation might be able to help with child care or meals, sitting with the dying person to give a family member a break, and helping with household tasks such as mowing the lawn, cleaning, or buying groceries.

7. Facilitate Anticipatory Grieving

- Anticipatory grieving has to do with the fourth "task of grieving" that I outlined in chapter 1, namely, *to adjust to a world in which the deceased is no longer physically present.* In Betty's story, the pastor is alert to signs of anticipatory grieving by Betty and family members. The key to and challenge of healthy anticipatory grieving is to prepare for a future absence of the physical presence of a loved one while simultaneously staying connected to this person in the present.

- The pastor helps Betty's family anticipate what the future would be like without her. In doing so, he helps them be aware of any unfinished remaining business, whether it be emotional, relational, practical, or financial. Betty was both sad and joyful as she wrote to her granddaughters letters that are to be opened on their wedding days.

8. Be Prepared to Be a Liaison among the Dying Person, Family, and Medical Personnel

- The patient and family may want the pastor to be with the dying person and family as they talk with medical personnel. Patients and family can be intimidated by medical staff. They may be embarrassed to ask questions. And they may not be able to concentrate on, understand, or remember details shared by doctors, nurses, and social workers when they are grieving. A pastor helps by being with the patient and family, by taking notes, by making sure the patient and family have understood what is being said, and by encouraging the patient and family to ask medical staff any questions.

- The pastor may need to advocate for the patient around matters of care. In doing so, the pastor respects the medical staff's professional competency and commitments to care. Unfortunately, in some institutions, elder abuse is an issue that pastors should be alert to but should not necessarily assume.

- Be attentive to needs of children. Some medical centers have rules that limit children's visitation. In the case of a dying patient, the pastor can sometimes encourage a relaxation of the rules so that children who are prepared can say their good-byes.

Pastors can encourage honest expressions of love and concern between the children and the dying person or recently deceased. If children are not allowed to visit or if the parents or children choose for them not to visit, the pastor talks honestly and genuinely with children and follows up with them about their grief.

- When a patient is actively dying in a hospital, the pastor often escorts family members between the waiting room and the patient's room to say their good-byes. The pastor, using sensitivity around issues of privacy, often stands outside the door while family members speak to the dying.

- Recognize that no one knows when death will occur. Though Betty died soon after life support was removed, sometimes people linger for days. If this is the case, the pastor can ask if there is any "unfinished business" with which the dying may be concerned. This happens even if the dying is in a coma. There may be an estranged loved one who needs to come say good-bye. Family members may need to "give permission" to the dying, saying that it is okay for the dying to leave this earth. The pastor, in talking with loved ones, can help name issues that may be causing the dying person to resist death.

- While being present in the death process, the pastor needs to exercise care for the family, respect for their privacy, and appropriate self-care and attention to other responsibilities through the process. Availability is key. Availability can be through physical presence or by phone when necessary.

9. Be Attentive to Intersections with God's Story

By being present with the dying and loved ones, the pastor listens for theological themes as they emerge throughout the process. These themes reflect and express theological meaning that the dying and grieving are making of this event. By attending to these expressions, the pastor facilitates theological meaning making of this life and death. In some cases, the grieving person openly articulates these intersections: "My dad is like Job. There's no one more kind or faithful than he. He does not deserve this suffering." Or, "The prodigal is finally going home." Other times, it may be appropriate for the pastor to name such intersections as he or she notices them. To help with this naming or identifying process, Paul Pruyser offers seven areas to which the pastor can be attuned. The following list shows these seven key areas that can help the pastor diagnose the theological meaning-making process in which the dying and grieving are engaged.[3] Pruyser outlines the sorts of questions pastors can be asking themselves as they reflect on their interactions with the dying and grievers:

- *Awareness of the Holy.* What is sacred to the individuals? What are their relationships to powers and forces beyond themselves? What do they see God doing in their midst?

- *Providence.* Is there a sense that life and afterlife are under God's guidance and therefore are trustworthy?

- *Faith.* Does faith and theological orientation help give meaning to life and death? Are there differing beliefs represented among the individuals? Throughout the dying and death process, the pastor can shape conversations around the beliefs of the dying/ deceased while being attentive to and respectful of the other faith stories present.

- *Grace or Gratefulness.* Is there a sense of worthiness in the individuals that allows them to receive the goodwill of others?

- *Repentance.* Is there a need for forgiveness to be voiced or received either between loved ones or from God? The pastor can listen for sorrow, remorse, or regret and allow for these emotions to be expressed and shared. The pastor can share the good news of the gospel and provide the assurance of God's forgiving love.

- *Communion.* Is there a sense of caring and being cared for by others (such as with family and the congregation)? Does a sense of community help reduce a sense of anxiety and alienation in the dying and death process?

- *Meaning.*[4] Is there a sense that the life that has been lived has been one of significance and will continue to be one of ongoing contribution? If so, how is meaning being made of this death and life?

Attention to these seven areas helps the pastor understand the ways the dying and grieving are making theological meaning of this person's life and death. Sensing the ways that the stories of the dying and grieving are intersecting with God's story informs pastoral care now and in the future as the funeral process continues to unfold.

Conclusion

In this chapter, we've looked at nine issues around effective pastoral care in the funeral-preparation process when it involves death after long-term illness or condition: (1) *respect and honor the sacred process of dying and death;* (2) *recognize that the funeral process begins before death;* (3) *take the office of pastor seriously;* (4) *attend to family systems;* (5) *help the dying person and the family prepare for death;* (6) *involve the congregation in care;* (7) *facilitate anticipatory grieving;* (8) *be prepared to be a liaison among the dying person, family, and medical personnel;* and (9) *be attentive to intersections with God's story.*

We have seen the ways that being with the dying person and the family can help facilitate grieving once the death occurs. In the next chapter, we move to sudden death. There you will find described the unique challenges of unexpected death and explore pastoral interventions that facilitate a good death and healthy grieving in the context of funeral preparation.

Chapter 3

Caring through Sudden Death

The previous chapter discussed pastoral responses to anticipated death. In this chapter, we discuss pastoral responses to sudden death.

Sudden death occurs in all sorts of ways. Section 1 gives various scenarios of the types of sudden death a pastor might encounter. Next, section 2 discusses features of sudden death. Then, section 3 offers a three-part A-B-C model for framing pastoral intervention in sudden-death situations. We conclude with a discussion of two specific scenarios involving cross-cultural ministry and suicide (section 4) while, throughout, attending to the intersections of the stories of the deceased, the grieving, the congregation, the pastor, and God, all of which comprise the funeral process.

1. Sudden-death Scenarios

Sonja's Story

Sonja and her husband, Tom, both African American, joined a mostly Caucasian church three months ago when Sonja was six months pregnant with their first child. A week before her due date, Sonja went to her prenatal checkup, where she learned that the baby had died in her womb. Sonja, devastated, called Tom, saying she was being admitted to the hospital, where she would deliver their stillborn daughter. Tom called the pastor. What does the pastor do?

George's Story

George, a forty-nine-year-old unchurched husband and father of three, called his wife, Karen, to say he was leaving work. When he didn't come home and didn't answer his phone, Karen drove to his office. She found George dead on his office floor. George's mother, Ruth, called her pastor from the hospital. What does the pastor do?

Nick's Story

Twenty-six-year-old Nick was in a head-on collision and was taken to the trauma bay of a Saint Louis hospital. At three a.m., the phone woke Nick's parents, Bob and Betty, in their home. Their son was in critical condition. Bob and Betty frantically drove four hours to the hospital to find that their son had died. They called their pastor. What does the pastor do?

Dorothy's Story

Dorothy, an eighty-five-year-old parishioner, did not answer her phone. Her daughter, Laurie, left work to check on her mom. Laurie was horrified to find Dorothy in her bathroom, dead and covered with blood. Laurie called the pastor of the church where Dorothy was a member, but where Laurie no longer attended. What does the pastor do?

Carrie's Story

Carrie and Scott started dating in youth group and married after college. A third-grade teacher, twenty-seven-year-old Carrie trained for marathons during summers. While Scott was at work, Carrie texted Scott to say she was going on a long run in the nearby state park. She never came home. Days later after an extensive search, police found her body in a shallow grave in the park. What does Carrie and Scott's pastor do?

Joe's Story

Ellen knew her twenty-one-year-old son, Joe, was depressed. He had been looking for a job for over a year. Two years ago, he was indicted on a felony count for selling marijuana. Joe's girlfriend, Annie, recently broke up with him. Ellen came home from work and found Joe's lifeless body hanging by a noose from a rafter. Ellen called her pastor. What does Ellen's pastor do?

Jack's Story

The sixth-grade class took an overnight trip to an outdoor skills and leadership camp two hours out of town. Shortly after lights out, an unpredicted tornado decimated the boys' cabin. Debris killed Jack, one of the students, instantly. Camp counselors called Jack's divorced parents, Jessie and Dave. Jessie's pastor, knowing about the school trip, heard about the tornado on the TV. What does the pastor do?

2. Features of Sudden Death

All of these stories demonstrate the shocking interruption of sudden death in people's lives. Though grief is not necessarily greater in sudden death than in anticipated death, sudden death does present particular challenges. Alan Wolfelt[1] defines sudden death as:

- Premature. Grievers perceive that a "normal life span" was cut short.

- Unexpected. Grievers had no time to prepare or anticipate the death or life without the deceased.

- Calamitous. Grievers' worlds are shattered by a death that seems tragic and senseless.

Accordingly, in situations of sudden death, grievers can experience:[2]

- A range of emotions, including anger, rage, guilt, fear, and depression. Grievers may quickly cycle through these emotions and/or experience many emotions simultaneously. Shock can delay grievers' cognitive functioning, making it difficult to process information.

- Intense anger. Anger is a sign of protest, a reaction against something that shouldn't have happened. Grievers may be angry at God, at the world, and even at the person who died.

- A diminished capacity to cope. Sudden loss is so disruptive that grievers can be overwhelmed by the loss.

- Different reactions to funeral preparations. Oftentimes, grievers have given no forethought to funeral preparations. For some, the funeral-preparation process may be anger provoking or overwhelming. Planning a funeral can be beyond an already overwhelmed state of mind. For others, it can also be a centering and

35

meaning-making process. In both cases, the pastor's guidance can be helpful.

- Difficulty in processing the implications of the death. Grievers often have limited capacity to make meaning out of their own life story, now interrupted by this sudden death.

- A need to process the reality of the death. Grievers often make sense of the death by giving a step-by-step account of what happened. They may tell and retell the story as they attempt to acknowledge that their loved one has actually died. Acknowledging the reality of death is the first "task of grieving."

- A desire to make sense of the senseless. Often sudden and traumatic loss violates a belief system: "This isn't how things are supposed to happen." "Why was such a good person's life cut so short?" "Nobody should have to die like this." The more traumatic and senseless the death, the more grievers search for some kind of meaning. In integrating the death story, the life story, the grievers' stories, and God's story in the funeral process, the pastor helps the grieving begin to make meaning of that which seems meaningless.

- "If only" thinking. Grievers often try to determine ways that the loss could have been prevented: "If only I had noticed the signs." "If only I had stopped him from going that night." "If only I hadn't said those words." "If only I had been with her." Grievers need to express their "if only's" without their feelings of helplessness being silenced.

- A feeling of incompleteness. With sudden death, grievers often feel that there is unfinished business. They regret all that could or should have been said and done. They regret the opportunity to resolve the past or to live into the future. The pastor addresses grievers' sense of unfinished business throughout the funeral process.

- The blame game. Some grievers blame the deceased: "Why was he driving at that hour of the night?" Other people blame grievers for what happened: "I can't believe her parents let her go to that party by herself." Blame, with its attendant judgment, distances grievers from networks of support.

- A sense of isolation. The rage, confusion, and depression of grief can cause grieving people not to want to be around others, or others not to want to be around them. Often, others do not know what to say to family members. Family members may feel uncomfortable interacting with others during the visitation and funeral services.

- A lack of security. As this sudden death is incorporated into grievers' meaning-making systems, some wait for the other shoe to drop, certain that "bad things happen in threes." Some grievers lose their belief in a benevolent world and gracious God. Fear and anxiety increase.

- A crisis in faith. As grievers attempt to make theological meaning in the face of sudden death, some question God's power, presence, and mercy. Some struggle, asking why God, who is all powerful, all merciful, and ever present, did not prevent this devastating loss. How will the pastor present God's story in the funeral service of one who died a tragic and seemingly meaningless death?

- A high level of functioning with little apparent emotional reaction. There are no cookie-cutter images of how people will or should respond to sudden or traumatic death. Shock and denial are protective mechanisms that allow people to assimilate the unthinkable slowly. Some grievers display little emotion in public. Throughout the funeral process, grievers need sensitive and appropriate care, not judgment.

Grievers, then, experience a wide range of responses to sudden death. With these responses, grievers unwittingly begin to engage the five "tasks of grieving," introduced in chapter 1, namely: (1) to accept the reality of the death, (2) to express grief around the death, (3) to make meaning of the deceased's life and death, (4) to adjust to a world in which the deceased is no longer physically present, and (5) to redefine the relationship with the deceased in terms of memory, legacy, and love. The pastor who companions grievers through this valley of grief gains their trust. Several approaches facilitate the pastor's appropriate expressions of care.

3. A-B-C Model for Pastoral Intervention in Sudden-death Situations

Recognizing the above challenges, here is a model to help frame pastoral response in sudden-death situations. Although there is no one correct way to respond to sudden death, there are, certainly, wrong ways to respond.

For instance, do not say:

- I know how you feel.
- She's in a better place.
- This is God's will.
- At least he's not suffering.
- God won't give you what you can't handle.

Rather, it is important for the pastor to have an adaptable model for appropriate pastoral intervention, one that is consistent with the rest of the funeral process. This three-part model is adapted from the A-B-C method, first formulated by psychiatrist Warren L. Jones[3] and used by many pastoral-care practitioners.[4] This adaptation is particularly appropriate for intersecting the five stories of the deceased, grievers, congregation, pastor, and God in sudden-death situations. The A-B-C model consists of three dimensions:

(A) **Attend** to immediate needs of those most affected by the death.

(B) **Be aware** of the situation and stories of other grievers, the congregation, the pastor, and God.

(C) **Carry out** commitments made through initial contact.

These dimensions are obviously connected. This method affords the opportunity to express appropriate pastoral care through this phase of the funeral process.

(A) Attend to Immediate Needs of Those Most Affected by the Death

The following discussion alerts a pastor to the kinds of things that may need immediate attention and the types of immediate responses that might be appropriate, depending on the varied situations of sudden death.

With sudden death, the pastor is usually, but not always, informed by a phone call. When the call comes:

- Assess the caller's needs. Is the caller who reported the death safe? Does she or he need to calm down so she or he can be understood? If so, the pastor can talk the person down with a calm but firm voice, possibly also suggesting that the caller take deep breaths. Have emergency personnel been notified? What are the immediate needs of others who are present?

- Do a quick self-check. Simultaneously, the pastor is doing a quick scan to examine her own availability, needs, and resources. "Is there anything that would prevent me from being fully present?" "Is there anyone else equipped to provide care in addition to or instead of me (associate minister? Stephen minister?)?" In rare cases, if the pastor has experienced a recent traumatic death similar to this one, she may not be emotionally available enough to provide care. If the deceased is not a church member, is the pastor able to be available?

- Start to chart those involved. Family and grieving situations are complex. By identifying family systems and dynamics, relational connections, and levels of closeness among the deceased and grievers, the pastor can better understand and facilitate interactions that promote healthy relating and grieving. In diagram form, the pastor can list the names, relationships, and phone numbers.

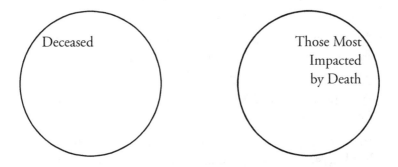

- Remember that all involved—the deceased, those most impacted by the death, the congregation, and the pastor—are sustained and connected by God's story that encircles them all and unfolds throughout the funeral process.

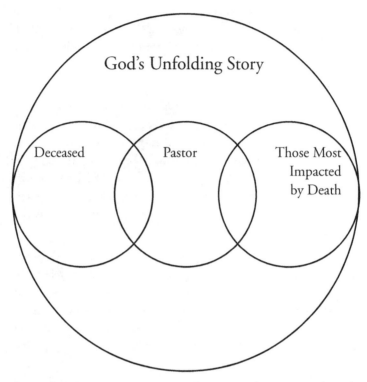

- Be a calm, nonanxious presence. Do not underestimate the value of being the calm in the midst of emotional storms.

- Use appropriate touch, such as reaching out to hug, to touch an arm, or to hold a hand. Touch can be calming to those in shock. If the pastor is unsure about touching, ask.

- Find a private physical setting. If possible, sit with the grievers to facilitate rapport.

- Attend to the grievers' physical needs—water, coffee, food, warm blankets, and tissues. Providing for needs helps grievers feel safe.

- Ask open-ended questions that focus on circumstances of the death:
    o What happened?
    o How did you learn of the death?
    o Where were you?
    o When was the last time you saw him or her?

- Use attentive body language. Lean in. Look into grievers' eyes. Nod to show you are listening. Let your physical responses mirror the grievers' so that they feel more connected to you. For example, match your breathing patterns to theirs and then slow your breathing. This helps calm grievers. Mirror the way they are sitting with your arms and legs.

- Listen with care.

- Receive emotions without judging.

- Offer empathetic responses:
    o How very sad.
    o This makes no sense.
    o How devastating.
    o Your whole world has collapsed.
    o Oh, this is awful.
    o So you are feeling like God has turned God's back on you.

- Accept anger toward God and other people involved in the situation. Don't defend God. This isn't the time to offer theological explanations. Grievers want to be heard. When grievers express their anger, they are less likely to act out behaviorally. The pastor not only hears the emotions in the moment but also engages them throughout the funeral process.

- If you fear physical violence from intense emotion, speak firmly to the griever that anger is fine, but violent behavior is not acceptable. If necessary, seek assistance from others.

- Do not force grievers to talk if they do not want to talk. It is okay simply to be with them in supportive silence.

- If organ or tissue donation is an option, medical personnel will discuss this with family. Consider being present in this conversation. Help mediate questions and differing positions. Frame options through the likely perspective of the deceased and the lens of faith. If the decision is made to donate organs, the pastor can remain with the family and provide a comforting and affirming presence.

- Anticipate that people experience death differently. You may need to assure some grievers that varied responses and feelings are normal and healthy. There is no one "correct" way to grieve.

- Determine key decision-makers and those who will want to give input into the funeral service. These are also the folk for whom the pastor will continue to provide care.

- Ask if there are any questions for medical personnel. The pastor can be present in the meeting, write down medical responses to questions, and ensure that all questions are sufficiently answered.

- Ask if grievers would like to see the body. Some will say yes; others will decline. Viewing the body helps confirm the reality of death, one of the tasks of grieving. Medical staff can make the body presentable. If grievers choose not to view the body at this stage, the pastor respects that decision, knowing that a viewing at the funeral home may be a possibility later. The body may need to be taken to a medical examiner, in which case visitation may be delayed.

- If grievers want to see the body, accompany them. Some cry; some scream; some hit the body in anger; some are simply silent. Encourage grievers to say good-byes or any final words.

- Offer to read a short scripture (e.g., Psalm 23), lead a favorite hymn, or pray with the family. Be brief and to the point. This is not the time for anything but simple, honest prayers. Also be careful not to "preach" during your prayer just to make yourself feel better or like you are "doing something." Ask grievers how they would like you to pray. Smart phones are a helpful resource for prayers, music, and Scripture. Ask the grievers if they would like to pray as well.

- Provide emotional support as family members complete required forms. A postmortem form is usually required to allow a hospital to release a body to a funeral home. If grievers are not ready to decide on a funeral home preference immediately, their selection can usually be called in to the hospital in the next twenty-four to forty-eight hours. Medical personnel will advise if this is contrary to their policy.

- Determine if the grievers are expecting you, the pastor, to do the funeral. Mostly this will be obvious; other times it will need to be made explicit. Make a time to meet with the family in the next day or two to talk about the funeral service. Have as many family members who want to have input into the funeral process present. Determine a time and place to meet.

- Accompany grievers to the funeral home if possible. Grievers may have theological questions about burial or cremation. Being present enables a pastor to offer support to grievers while also coordinating funeral arrangements with the funeral director. See chapter 4 for more on funeral-service preparations.

- Assess whether grievers have adequate resources for the next twenty-four to forty-eight hours.
    - o Do they have support and presence from family and friends?
    - o Are they capable of driving, or do they need a ride or a cab?
    - o Are there others in the congregation who can provide support?
    - o It is helpful when leaving the hospital or funeral home to walk the grievers to their cars to show additional support and care.

With these issues and questions in mind, the pastor attends to those most affected by the death.

(B) Be Aware of the Stories of Other Grievers, the Congregation, the Pastor, and God

Now that the pastor has attended to the situations of those most affected, the second dimension in this A-B-C model for pastoral intervention involves the pastor being aware of other grievers and the congregation, if applicable, and the pastor's own responses and emotions. These stories are also located in the context of God's story of loving presence and future hope.

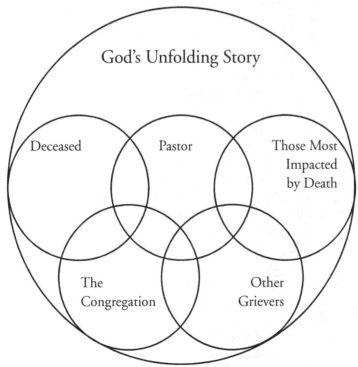

God's Unfolding Story

Deceased

Pastor

Those Most Impacted by Death

The Congregation

Other Grievers

As the pastor becomes aware of these further stories, she is alert to ministry opportunities and ways these various stories intersect.

- Other Grievers. As the pastor talks with those most affected by the death, she is able to identify who these grievers are and the larger family system.
    - o Are there children? Stepchildren? Parents? An ex-spouse? Friends? Divorced parents? The pastor begins to map the family system, noting names and contact numbers.
    - o Did the deceased have strained or broken relationships? Can the pastor facilitate steps toward healing?
    - o Funerals, like weddings, are prime occasions for family skeletons and conflicts to emerge. Strained and broken relationships can significantly affect reactions among grievers and can affect the decision-making process. Expecting reconciliation is oftentimes too much, but the pastor works toward civility.
    - o What social, vocational, professional, volunteer, and hobby-related circles did the deceased participate in? How will these folks be alerted about the death?
    - o Are there people who live far away who need to connect with the family and grievers? Enter names and contact information onto your map.
- The Congregation. When sudden death involves a church member, it affects the congregation.
    - o Talk with the closest grievers about what sort of information they want disseminated and how. Respect their privacy.
    - o Are there congregational groups who will be especially affected by this death? Sunday school class? Committee? Choir? Youth group? How will these groups be informed?
    - o Activate the congregation's prayer chain. Will the pastor begin this process, with the family's permission? How much information will be circulated?
    - o Is there a grief care system in place to be activated? Stephen ministers to be called to minister to the grieving?
    - o Are there others in the congregation who have experienced similar trauma that might helpfully be able to support the family?
    - o If the funeral will be in the church, what organizational or scheduling matters need attention? Who will be involved—

music director, organist, coordinator of funeral dinners, custodian, sound technician, and so on?

   o Will the pastor address the sudden death from the pulpit in worship beyond soliciting the congregation's prayers?

• The pastor. Be attentive to how this situation is affecting you as pastor.

   o What feelings or memories is this triggering in you?
   o Is this evoking any of your own grief experiences?
   o Do you need additional support?
   o How will you debrief?
   o If you are close to the deceased, how are you processing your own grief?

• God. While being present with grievers and attending to congregational dimensions, the pastor listens for emerging theological themes and experiences of God. These themes reflect and express theological meaning that the grieving and members of the congregation are making of this event. As outlined in chapter 2, being aware of the following seven themes identified by Paul Pruyser[5] provides the pastor with areas to attend to during this immediate crisis and throughout the grieving process.

   o *Awareness of the Holy.* Do grievers see God anywhere in this situation? Do they blame or resist God? Are they aware of God's sustaining care in the midst of the shock and violence? What do they see God doing in this situation?

   o *Providence.* Is there any awareness of God's presence? Do they perceive God as being negligent or powerless? Or do they sense God's care even in these devastating circumstances?

   o *Faith.* What questions of faith and faithfulness are being asked? Are some grievers employing faith clichés that do not match their emotional states? Can the pastor encourage honest, multivalent expressions of pain, doubt, and belief, all of which are consistent with faith experiences? Can the pastor provide assurances of God's faithfulness despite appearances to the contrary?

   o *Grace or Gratefulness.* Is there any awareness of God's grace in this situation? Do they see the death as a punishment and as a withholding of God's grace? Can they receive expressions of care and support? Are feelings of devastation and blame dominating? Do they give thanks for a life well lived—even if it is a life cut short?

o *Repentance.* Is there a need for forgiveness to be voiced, extended, or received involving any of those involved—the deceased, grievers, or God? Allow for expressions of sorrow, remorse, and regret. Can the pastor dwell with the grievers in the dark reality of their Good Friday before rushing to the hope of the resurrection? Yet also, can the pastor express assurances of God's forgiving love as appropriate?

o *Communion.* What community exists to support grievers? What can the pastor do to make connections and increase communal support? Can grievers receive it?

o *Meaning.*[6] What meaning are the grievers creating about the death? Does meaninglessness or despair dominate? Are grievers and the congregation formulating redeeming acts of goodness, such as requesting contributions to Mothers Against Drunk Drivers in the wake of a drunk-driving accident?

Being attentive to these themes and questions helps the pastor assess perspectives throughout the whole funeral process. But the pastor must be careful. Notice what grievers are actually expressing rather than prescribe what they *should* be expressing. Noticing what grievers are expressing helps the pastor do ministry at the points of intersection among grievers' stories and God's story of loving presence and future hope.

Especially appropriate for the crisis of sudden death are the language and emotions of lament.[7] In the biblical tradition, lament is an appeal for divine help in the midst of distress. A lament voices complaint or protest to God and demands that God answer: "How long, O LORD? Will you forget me forever? How long will you hide your face from me? How long must I bear pain in my soul, and have sorrow in my heart all day long?" (Psalm 13:1-2).

There are numerous psalms of lament, such as Psalms 13, 22, and 42, as well as lament in Lamentations and Job 3. Walter Brueggemann has identified the central dynamic of psalms of lament as one of orientation, disorientation, and new orientation.[8] Disorientation results from disrupting the normal. In disorientation, people express to God their profound feelings of loss, devastation, loneliness, injustice, and pain, including the pain of God's silence or hiddenness. The language of lament shows that the biblical tradition does not silence raw voices of anguish and despair.

In addition to naming the emotions of disorientation, lament psalms move through a process toward a new orientation based in God's faithful and transforming presence. Hope for the future emerges from and in the cries of lament as the psalms move from plea to praise. Hope comes from experiencing God's healing, transformation, and redemption.

Lament psalms often have a communal dimension to them. Grievers need others who will stand with them in the valley of the shadow. They need others who will "hear" their cries of lament and pain while also bearing the hope that healing will someday come. The pastor's role is not to fix the griever but to stand with the griever and "companion them" in their lament.

(C) Carry out Commitments

Having (A) attended to immediate needs of those most affected, and (B) become aware of the situation and stories of other grievers, the congregation, the pastor, and God's unfolding story, the pastor is care-full to attend to the third part of the A-B-C model: (C) carrying out any commitments she or he has made throughout the process.

Having a system helps the pastor keep track of these commitments concerning arrangements that she or he has made through the process. Systems might include:

- A three-ring binder with funeral materials including checklists, templates, phone numbers and addresses, a directory of area funeral homes and grief support services, congregational resources, and lists of resources (see appendix in this book).

- A chart for contact information that allows the pastor to document relationships, names, and numbers of different participants in the funeral process (grievers most affected, other grievers, congregation, funeral director, and so on) (see appendix).

- Electronic files accessed from smart phones, tablets, and so on.

- Small spiral notebooks or 3x5 cards that can be carried in a pocket or purse.

Having a system helps a pastor plan to be organized in the midst of complex needs and apparent chaos. A pastor's care-full follow-through helps grievers know that the pastor is a secure base in what feels like an insecure world. The pastor's thoughtful follow-up responses help represent God's loving presence and future hope.

Though every sudden-death situation is different, and all grievers experience death and grief differently, the A-B-C system—**a**ttending to those most affected by death; **b**eing aware of other grievers' stories, the congregational story, the pastor's story, and God's story; and **c**arrying out commitments—offers a flexible, yet focused framework for providing pastoral care as part of the funeral process in situations of sudden death.

4. Two Important Scenarios

To conclude this chapter, here are the particular dynamics of two of the scenarios that began our chapter, namely, cross-cultural ministry and suicide. Each has its own specific challenges, as grievers engage the same five tasks of grieving: (1) to accept the reality of the death; (2) to express grief around the death; (3) to make meaning of the deceased's life and death; (4) to adjust to a world in which the deceased is no longer physically present; and (5) to redefine the relationship with the deceased in terms of memory, legacy, and love.

Cross-cultural Ministry

Sonja's story precipitates the question of how a white male pastor will minister to an African American woman and her husband. This is a complicated situation involving both cross-cultural pastoral care and issues related to stillbirth, so what follows is only an overview.

In cross-cultural situations, the story approach to the funeral process creates a bridge between differences. Connection is made by the pastor's willingness to assume a position of not knowing. Rather than presenting oneself as having all the answers, the pastor is present to hear the stories of the grievers and thereby learn from them how to facilitate grieving and shape the funeral process appropriately.

In his discussion of pastoral care and African American culture, Edward Wimberly names this approach *story-listening* and says that it is "an important dimension of African American pastoral care."[9] Wimberly says that the story-listening approach involves "empathically hearing the story of the person involved in life struggles. Being able to communicate that the person in need is cared for and understood is a result of attending to the story of the person as he or she talks."[10] Drawing from the Sonja and Tom scenario, then, story-listening includes:

- *Showing humility.* The pastor says to Sonja, "As a man, I can't imagine what it must feel like to give birth to your dead baby. I wonder what this experience is like for you." And to Tom, "I can't even imagine what you are feeling right now."

- *Allow the suffering ones to teach you.* The pastor says, "Tell me what would be most helpful to you right now."

- *Lead from the heart.* As the pastor hears and empathizes with Sonja and Tom's feelings, they feel cared for and supported in their expressions of grief.

- *Follow their lead.* After Sonja gave birth to her stillborn baby, she wanted her extended family to be with them. As Sonja, Tom, and other family members took turns holding baby Rebekah's dead body, the family cried loud wails. The pastor, not used to such intense expressions of emotion, allowed himself to be comfortable in his discomfort. He heard their stories and expressions of their pain. He felt tears well up in his own eyes. After a while, he asked if they wanted prayer, which they did. Sonja and Tom named prayer requests. The pastor prayed and then asked if they had a song they would like to sing. As Sonja rocked her dead baby in her arms, everyone held hands and sang "Swing Low, Sweet Chariot."

- *Attend to all grievers.* The pastor cared for Sonja and Tom and other family members. He leaned down and listened to nieces and nephews, hearing their sadness about their cousin. He listened to Sonja and Tom's parents' pain at the death of their first grandchild.

- *Help facilitate connections.* The pastor told Sonja and Tom of others in the congregation who have suffered the loss of a child, offering to connect them. Sonja and Tom were interested. Subsequently, he carried out this commitment by connecting the couples.

- *Map relationships and document contact information.* Write down names, relationships, and phone numbers in your established system. See appendix for template.

The pastor engages in Edward Wimberly's "story-listening approach," humbly willing to learn and be instructed in expressing appropriate care. This approach resonates with the "companioning" model discussed in chapter 1. To learn more about cross-cultural pastoral care, see Wimberly's *African American Pastoral Care* (Nashville: Abingdon Press, 2008),

Emmanuel Lartey's *In Living Color: An Intercultural Approach to Pastoral Care and Counseling* (New York: Jessica Kingsley Publishers Ltd, 2003), and R. Esteban Montilla and Ferney Medina's *Pastoral Care and Counseling with Latino/a*s (Minneapolis: Fortress, 2006).[11]

Pastor Khalebb Ramirez suggests things a pastor should know when ministering with Latinos:

- *Establish an environment of safety, trust, and respect.* This will allow the family to feel they are not betraying the unwritten family code about loyalty.

- *The family is the main source of support, care, guidance, and healing.* Problems and conflicts should stay within the family.

- *Identify and respect the person in a position of authority.*

- *Females often make decisions about funeral arrangements.*

- *Family solidarity is very important during the decision-making process.*

- *Latinos often express emotion openly.*

- *Faith is about relationship and intimacy with the transcendent, the self, and others.* Faith helps make sense of their existence.

- *The community/congregation is a source of strength and resources for assisting the family.*

- *Most important are the pastor's warmth, empathy, genuine interest, and love for others.*[12]

Suicide

Joe's story precipitates the question around the special needs of suicide grievers. There are varied responses to suicide, as with any death. There are, though, some important features to be noted:[13]

- Loved ones of a suicide victim often feel more guilt, anger, and bewilderment than if their loved one had died another kind of death. The pastor listens to these emotions and receives them without judgment. Expressing grief is one of the basic tasks or grieving.

- Grievers may feel they had some blame in the death. As grievers attempt to make meaning of the suicide, they may feel regret and remorse over aspects of the relationship before the person died. The pastor, while assuring that suicide is not a griever's fault, can listen for the need for God's forgiveness.

- Some grievers may feel relief. The pastor encourages the expression of all emotions, another task of grieving.

- Often, in suicide, there is a tendency to focus largely on the way the deceased died. Throughout the funeral process, the pastor helps grievers incorporate the death story into a broader life story, all of which is in the context of God's healing story.

- In some grievers, there may be a denial that the death was, in fact, a suicide, especially if no note is found. It is best not to try to break through the denial but to allow grievers to accept the reality in their own time through the grief.

- Be aware that the grieving process for suicide deaths is more complex and difficult and that the healing process takes longer than when a death, even though painful, is expected.

In Joe's story, the pastor met with Ellen at the hospital the night she found his body. When Annie, Joe's former girlfriend, appeared, Ellen was initially upset. Ellen initially resented her presence, blaming their breakup as a possible cause. The pastor helped them name and talk through their complex emotions. Annie's obvious grief and guilt softened Ellen's reaction, and the two hugged tightly. The pastor listened carefully to both Ellen and Annie's intense feelings of guilt. She affirmed their swirl of emotions, acknowledged their guilt and pain, and affirmed their love for Joe that embraced his brokenness. The pastor did not seek to provide answers but joined them in their questions. She accompanied Ellen and Annie in the valley of the shadow of their devastation, knowing that God is also caring for them.

Annie and Ellen's grief stories were different. Because Joe's body had already been taken to the medical examiner and Annie could not see Joe's body, she initially had trouble accepting the reality of his death. Ellen couldn't get the vision of her son's hanging out of her mind. The pastor listened empathetically for as long as they wanted to talk. Soon, both Ellen's and Annie's parents arrived, and the pastor realized that they were in good care. She arranged to meet with Ellen and Annie the next morning to begin planning the funeral service. In her notebook, the pastor wrote a reminder to find out about suicide support groups in the area so as to offer this resource to Ellen and Annie.

Conclusion

In this chapter, features and experiences of sudden-death situations were introduced and described. Additionally, a three-part A-B-C model for framing pastoral intervention for sudden-death situations was detailed. Throughout the chapter, intersections among stories of the deceased, the grieving, the congregation, and the pastor, all in the context of God's loving, gracious presence, were illustrated. In the next two chapters, we turn to the pastor's task of creating a meaningful funeral service.

Chapter 4

Meeting with Family before the Funeral Service

This chapter has three sections. The first section focuses on the family meeting and suggests that the pastor's caring questions and empathetic responses can help the family tell stories about the deceased, express their grief, and make decisions about the visitation, funeral/memorial, and/or committal service. Throughout this process, the pastor assists the family in the five tasks of grieving. In the second section, in preparation for chapters 5 and 6, we'll discuss the functions of funerals. In section 3, we'll see how these functions are achieved through the intersections of the stories of the deceased, the grieving, the congregation, the pastor, and God. The intersections of these stories will inform the creation of the service and sermon.

1. Meeting with the Family

When the pastor meets with the family regarding funeral preparations, ideally this is not their first meeting. In a perfect world, the pastor has cared for the dying and the family throughout the dying process in situations of anticipated death (chapter 2), or the pastor has cared for the family in the aftermath of traumatic death (chapter 3). The pastor has then arranged with the family to have family members and close friends present to prepare for the funeral service. Though this process is desirable, we know that the world is not perfect. Especially given time restraints around funerals, pastors and families do the best they can.

There are three purposes for the pastor's meeting with the family prior to the funeral service:

(1) to care for family in a way that facilitates the five tasks of grieving,

(2) to gain insights and information that will be relevant to the service and sermon (to be discussed in chapters 5 and 6).

(3) to make decisions regarding the funeral service.

The pastor's first concern is caring for the family in their grief. Although grief is experienced in individual ways, grievers share common tasks of grieving, described in chapter 1. These tasks are:

(1) to accept the reality of the death.

(2) to express grief around the death.

(3) to make meaning of the deceased's life and death.

(4) to adjust to a world in which the deceased is no longer physically present.

(5) to redefine the relationship with the deceased in terms of memory, legacy, and love.

The pastor, by asking thoughtful questions and offering empathetic responses in the family meeting, helps those present address these tasks of grieving. As family members tell stories about the life and death of the deceased, they engage these tasks. They confront the reality of the death, express grief, and make meaning that will shape the funeral service and sermon, as well as shape their own future stories. Central to this meaning-making activity are the intersections among the lives of the grievers and the deceased. I use the plural term *intersections* because the memories and experiences of grievers will differ from one another.

The pastor facilitates further intersections and meaning making by helping grievers also make theological meaning of the deceased's life and death and of their own lives beyond this death. The pastor does so by listening for, and asking about, intersections with God's story in the life and death of the deceased and in the experience of the grievers. The following questions are suggestions for possible "story starters." These are suggestions and not intended to be worked like a laundry list of things meticulously to check off. These are suggestions of the types of questions to ask to encourage story sharing, meaning making, and intersections among the various stories.

These story starters fall into four categories, namely, those concerning the grievers, those concerning the life story of the deceased, those concerning thanksgiving for the deceased, and those concerning God's story.

Story Starters Concerning the Grievers

- It's been two days since Tyler died. How are you coping with all of this?
- Do you need anything that I can help you with?
- I understand that you, Sarah, were there when she died. Tell us about what happened.
- How did you hear about the death?
- Where were you when you learned about the death?
- When did you last see Frank?
- What did you talk about?
- Do you feel you had a chance to say good-bye?
- Does anything remain to be said?
- What will sustain you through this difficult loss?

Story Starters Concerning the Life Story of the Deceased

- Tell me about your father's life.
- When was he at his best?
- What were moments of courage in John's life?
- What did your brother like to read?
- What kind of music did your grandpa listen to?
- Who influenced your mother the most?
- Tell me about Mary's legacy, in terms of her influence in forming who you are.
- What stories did your grandma often repeat?
- Of what was she most proud?
- What were some of your sister's struggles and challenges?
- What did your aunt overcome?

- Can you describe some crossroads that your father faced and what he ultimately chose?

- What was Sean afraid of?

- What did he think was funny about life or about people?

- What gave Helen's life meaning?

- What causes was your daughter passionate about?

- What were your uncle's interests and hobbies?

- Are there any causes your father believed in that you'd like to continue?

- What did hope look like for your mother, especially at the end of life?

- No person is perfect. What were some of your brother's idiosyncrasies?

- What made Angie laugh?

- What were some of your grandfather's favorite memories?

- What are some of your favorite memories?

- How will his memory or spirit live on?

Story Starters Concerning Thanksgiving for the Deceased

- What was your mother particularly thankful for?

- What are you thankful for about her life?

- Is there anything in her dying or death experience for which you give thanks?

- How was your mom a blessing to you?

Story Starters Concerning God's Story (in Relation to Both the Deceased and the Grievers)

- What were your grandmother's faith beliefs?

- Tell me about your son's faith journey.

- What were your aunt's favorite hymns or songs?

- What were your father's favorite scriptures?

• In what ways did your mother feel God's presence as she was living or dying?

• How have you experienced God's presence throughout your mother's dying process?

• How has God comforted you, or how would you like to experience God's comfort, love, and peace?

• What does hope look like for your family?

• Do you have any questions?

By asking these sorts of questions, the pastor accomplishes the first two tasks of the meeting. She or he helps grievers address the tasks of grieving. She or he also gains significant insights from the intersection of stories and the meaning-making process that will inform the funeral service and sermon.

The third purpose of the meeting is to make decisions around the funeral service. The pastor needs to be aware that various scenarios are possible at this point. It could be that the family has already met with the funeral director and made several decisions. In this case, the family will need to share pertinent information with the pastor. It may also be that the deceased has preplanned the funeral. If this is the case, the pastor can help ensure that the funeral service will honor the deceased's wishes while also helping grievers address the tasks of grieving. Sometimes there can be tensions at this point. The pastor helps negotiate these tensions in the light of the multiple functions of the funeral, which are discussed in section 2 of this chapter.

It may also be that the family is meeting with the pastor prior to meeting with the funeral director. In this case, the pastor can help the family think through basic decisions, such as whether the family prefers burial or cremation. Another possibility is that the funeral director joins with this meeting. This option allows the pastor, funeral director, and family to coordinate aspects of the service together.

It is essential that the pastor and funeral director coordinate with each other around the family's decisions. See the appendix for a funeral service template for the pastor to share with funeral home directors.

Issues around Disposal of the Body

One issue a family needs to discuss concerns disposal of the body. This may be something that the family has already decided, or it may require exploration. Be prepared to discuss theological implications of cremation. Most

Christians accept cremation as a perfectly acceptable alternative to burial. Cremated bodies can be transformed and glorified just as buried bodies: "It is sown a physical body, it is raised a spiritual body" (1 Corinthians 15:44).

- If burial:
    o Where will the body be buried?

- If cremation:
    o Does the family want the body to be viewed at visitation and the funeral before cremation?
    o Will the cremated remains be placed in an urn or a box?
    o Where will the cremated remains be committed? Memorial garden? Columbarium? Scattered at a special place?

Issues around Service Preferences

A second issue that needs to be discussed concerns the family's preference for what kind of service(s) will take place. There are three types of funeral services.

(1) Does the family want a visitation? The visitation can be held at the funeral home, church, or home. Often informal, the gathering is often held the afternoon or evening before the funeral, memorial, or committal service. An advantage of a visitation is that it helps grievers with the tasks of grieving. Especially if the body or cremated remains are present, it helps grievers address the grieving task of *accepting the reality of the death*. The informal gathering allows grievers to address the grieving task of *expressing grief around the death*. When photos and memorabilia of the deceased's interests and contributions are present, the visitation helps grievers address the tasks of *redefining the relationship around memories, legacy, and love* and *adjusting to a world in which the deceased is no longer physically present*. A possible disadvantage is that a family may not have the energy to have an additional service.

(2) Does the family want a funeral or memorial service? Usually held at the church sanctuary or in the funeral home chapel, a traditional funeral is a formal service with the deceased's body present in a casket or the deceased's cremated remains present in an urn. The funeral is usually held within several days of death and is often preceded or followed by a graveside service if there is a body or cremated remains to be buried. A memorial service is similar to a funeral with the difference being that the deceased's body is not present. An urn with the deceased's cremated remains may or may not be present. A

memorial service is often less formal than a funeral and can take place at any time. When thoughtfully prepared, both the funeral and the memorial service facilitate all five tasks of grieving. We will discuss this further in chapter 5, "Creating the Funeral Service."

(3) Does the family want a committal service? This brief service involves committing a body or ashes to God in its final place of rest. The final resting place can be a gravesite, columbarium, mausoleum, memorial garden, or another place where family chooses to scatter the ashes of the deceased. A committal service can precede or follow a funeral, or it can be the only service. The committal service graphically expresses the finality of the deceased's death. In doing so, it facilitates the grievers' tasks around accepting the reality of the death and expressing grief around the death.

In discussing these options, the pastor attends to details around each of these particular types of services. I offer the following questions in order to highlight the range of matters that might need consideration.

Issues Concerning Visitation

- What is the time and place? (If likely attendees are older and retired, an afternoon visitation may be preferable.)
- Will a casket be present? Will it be open or closed?
- Will an urn be present?
- Will the family be displaying photos, memorabilia, a video, or a slide show?
- Does the family want music, candles, or flowers? Does the family want a guest book or note cards for attendees to write a memory and place in a basket?
- Will there be food and drink?

Issues Concerning Funeral*/Memorial Service (*=funeral only)

- Where will the service be held? Church? Funeral home? Other?
- Will the body and casket be present for the service?*
  - o Will the body need to be transported from the funeral home to the service location?*

o Does the family want to process with the casket or be seated ahead of time?*

o If there is a processional, who are the six to eight pall-bearers?* (Pallbearers can be female as well as male.)

o Will the casket be open or closed during the funeral service (it is usually closed)?*

o Will a pall cover the casket?* A pall is a special piece of cloth that covers the coffin. When the pall is white, it symbolizes the person's baptism.

o Will family assist with the placing of the pall, or shall it be placed by the funeral director?*

• Will an urn and cremated remains be present for the service?

o Will there be a processional with the urn?

o Will there be honorary pallbearers to accompany the urn?

o Does the family want to process with the urn or be seated ahead of time?

• Will the pastor ride to the cemetery in the hearse with the funeral director?*

• Will there be a military presence?

• Will there be a guest book?

• Does the family want to display photos or memorabilia or play a slide show or video with music before or after the service?

• Will bulletins be printed?

• Does the family have an obituary?

• Should the obituary be included in the bulletin?

• Are there particular scriptural passages that you would like included in the service?

• Are there other readings or poems that you would like included in the service?

• Are there hymns or songs that you would like included in the service?

• Will Communion be served?

• What musicians are requested (organist, choir, soloist, or other musicians)?

- What congregational resources are available for the funeral (choir, organist, other musicians, sound system for recorded music, or meal after the service)?

- What fees/honoraria are involved? Often, the funeral will build these costs into the total bill. Coordinate with the funeral director.
    - o Organist? _____
    - o Soloist or other music? _____
    - o Altar servers? _____
    - o Church? _____
    - o Pastor? _____

- What hymns or music would the family like included in the service (see the appendix for options)?

- Are there particular scriptures that the family would like included?

- Are there family members or friends who will want to speak about the deceased in the service? How do the family and pastor feel about this? Will the speakers be arranged in advance, or will there be an open microphone? Pastors often encourage speakers to be brief and to prepare scripts in advance.

- Will children be present? Unless there are strong objections, it is helpful for children also to address the tasks of grieving by attending funeral services.

- Is there a need for child care for younger children? Do congregational resources allow this option?

- Are there any rituals specific to the deceased's life and interests that can help family and friends make meaning of the life and death? See chapter 5 for discussion.

Issues Concerning a Committal Service

- Will the committal occur before or after a funeral or memorial service? Or will this be the only service?

- How many chairs are needed for family?

- Will elderly family members and grievers be able to access the grave?

- Will earth, sand, or water be used in the ceremony?

In this meeting with the family, the pastor facilitates the grief process of making meaning of the death, gains insights and information, and makes decisions regarding the funeral service. The pastor then uses information and insights gained from this meeting to create a meaningful funeral service and sermon that express the intersections of the stories of God, the deceased, the grievers, the congregation, and the pastor. To an understanding of a meaningful funeral service, we now turn.

2. Toward the Funeral: Functions of the Funeral

What makes a meaningful funeral? In this section, I use the term *funeral* expansively to include the three forms of service just discussed, namely, visitation, funeral/memorial, and committal services. I am suggesting that the creation of a funeral service and sermon happens at the intersections of the five stories.

There are different ways to understand the functions of funerals. On one end of the spectrum are those who think that the overriding function of funerals is to comfort the grievers. This approach says that funerals are "for the family." Herbert Anderson and Edward Foley, for example, argue that "every ritual moment in the funeral process should be evaluated in the light of its effect on the process of grieving."[1] That is, this viewpoint approaches funeral services primarily as an opportunity for pastoral care for grieving people.

On the other end of the spectrum are those who believe that the overriding function of funerals is to worship God. William Willimon states, "Against the definition of the purpose of a funeral as being 'for the family,' I argue that the purpose is the same as for any service of Christian worship: to worship God."[2] According to Thomas Long, "The purpose of a Christian funeral is to . . . enact the human obligation to care for the dead in such a way that we retell the story of baptism."[3] A funeral, he says, has the primary purpose (along with other purposes) of being kerygmatic:

> A good funeral, whatever else it may do, tells the kerygma, the gospel story. The funeral is bold to proclaim that, though it may appear that death has claimed yet another victim, the truth is that the one who has died has been raised to a new life in Christ and is now gathered with the saints in communion with God.[4]

That is, this viewpoint approaches funerals primarily as an opportunity to focus on God in worship and proclamation.

In the middle of the spectrum are those who believe that a funeral can serve multiple functions.[5]

62

Functions of Funerals

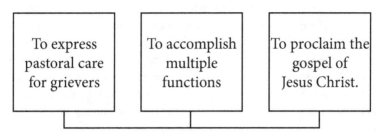

| To express pastoral care for grievers | To accomplish multiple functions | To proclaim the gospel of Jesus Christ. |

I join with those who see the funeral as serving multiple functions. Against those who argue for worship of God as the funeral's main function, I suggest that worship is but one of the dimensions, equal to and not greater than others. Although the funeral is a worship service, all worship is contextual. A funeral is a specific kind of worship service, one in which everyone present—the "assembled grievers"—is touched in some way by the life and death of the deceased. In this context, then, a funeral has three equally important functions.

One function of funerals, then, is to represent the deceased's life and death. Partly this is about honoring the deceased. But it involves much more. This person, created in the image of God, formed by God in his or her mother's womb, had a life story with a beginning and an end, a life story that is part of God's story of loving presence and future hope. A funeral represents the story of this person's life and death. That is, it *re-presents* the person's identity as a child of God who is embraced in God's love and is returning to God's eternal presence. The funeral re-presents this person in the context of worship, in the company of the people of God. This person may be mother, sister, daughter, aunt, friend, or whoever. And though these relationships continue to be very important, the first function of the funeral recognizes and celebrates this identity of the deceased as a child of God who is created in the image of God and who is now in the company of the saints of God.

A second function of funerals emerges from the fact that the deceased's story intersects with the stories of family and other grievers. These folks constitute the "assembled grievers" for the funeral. Each worshiper has been affected by the deceased's life or death story in particular ways. Each person brings a vast array of possible emotions, spanning hurt, loss, fear, relief, devastation, pride, numbness, isolation, celebration, shock, anger, denial, confusion, and disillusionment. These emotions may include feeling betrayed by God or a sense of God's presence or absence or powerlessness in not averting the death. The assembled bring these emotions into the presence of God. It is in this context that worship occurs.

This second function of the funeral, then, is to care for the assembled grieving gathered for worship and to help them to address the tasks of grieving. To care for grievers is to help them acknowledge this death and to put the life and death of the deceased into their own story. To care for grievers is to hear, name, and acknowledge their feelings before God. To care for grievers is to help them make meaning of the death and face a future without the physical presence of the deceased. That is, this second function of funerals takes seriously the context in which this particular form of worship of God takes place and takes seriously the tasks of grieving that the assembled grievers engage.

We see the same context exhibited in lament psalms. These psalms begin with God's people crying out to God in situations of loss and disorientation:

> My God, my God, why have you
>   forsaken me?
>   Why are you so far from
>   helping me, from the words
>   of my groaning?
> O my God, I cry by day, but you
>   do not answer;
>   and by night, but find no rest. (Psalm 22:1-2)

> Out of the depths I cry to you,
>   O LORD.
>   Lord, hear my voice!
> Let your ears be attentive
>   to the voice of my
>   supplications! (Psalm 130:1-2)

Lament psalms begin with these human experiences of brokenness and grief. The psalms locate these emotions of grief as part of a journey, which moves worshipers eventually to a very different experience of God. The lament psalms do not utter their concluding expressions of trust, praise, and hope in God without first embracing the pain and grief of the worshipers. To take up the experiences of grievers into God's loving, sustaining, hopeful presence is an important aspect of care for them that the funeral service performs.

Though grievers may feel abandoned by the deceased or by God, the Christian funeral affirms that each griever is held in the light of community and congregation of God's people. That is, this caring for grievers involves the gathering of a people. These assembled grievers become the congregation that joins together to sustain one another, to express grief, and to offer praise and thanksgiving to God for the life of the deceased. To care for grievers is to let them know that they are not alone. As the lament psalm proclaims: "I will tell of your name to my brothers and sisters; in the midst of the congregation I will praise you" (Psalm 22:22).

A third function of funerals is to proclaim God's good news of loving presence and future hope. It is in this worshipful context, of re-presenting the deceased as a child of God and caring for assembled grievers, that God is encountered. God's good news is not proclaimed in isolation from crying out to God in the face of death and hopelessness. It is precisely because of the crying out to God that the psalmist is able to praise God and proclaim God's presence, comfort, and faithfulness: "For he did not despise or abhor the affliction of the afflicted; he did not hide his face from me, but heard when I cried to him" (Psalm 22:24).

The funeral becomes the bridge that connects God's people—in whatever emotional state they are in—to the promise of God's loving presence, comfort, and hope. The funeral declares in the face of death the paradox that nothing separates the deceased or the grievers from the love of God. This good news reassures the congregation that the deceased is embraced in the ever-loving and never-ending presence of God. In their expression of grief, they can experience God in a deeper, more significant way. God's love and hope help make meaning of the deceased's life and death in that all is recognized to be in the context of God's loving story. Even when it does not seem apparent or make any sense to us, in God's story there is hope for reconciliation and new life. In the gathering of the community and the good news of God's abiding presence, the grieving congregation finds courage to live as God's children into an unknown future. The good news evokes the communion of saints among whom the deceased now abides and with whom grievers are connected by memory, legacy, and love.

3. Intersecting the Five Stories

As mentioned throughout, the funeral process involves the intersections of five stories: those of the deceased, the grieving, the congregation, and the pastor in the context of God's story. The question now becomes, *how does the pastor intersect these stories in accomplishing the three functions of the funeral?* She has heard the stories of the deceased. She knows the grief stories of the family and grieving. She knows the effect that the death of the person has had on the church congregation. The pastor knows her own grief over the death.

I am suggesting that the intersections of these five stories involve three key elements. The first element is the expression of grief in diverse forms. A second comprises expressions of thanksgiving and praise to God for the life of the deceased, even in the most tragic circumstances of sudden death. A third involves encounter with the good news of God's loving presence and future hope in the midst of these circumstances. These are illustrated in the diagram below.

These three elements of grief, thanksgiving, and God's good news are found in each of the stories:

- *The Deceased's Story.* The pastor can know something of the deceased's grief, thanksgiving, and experience of God from two possible sources. The first source is the pastor's own possible experience of the deceased either during the process of dying or in the course of normal pastoral work and social interactions before the deceased died. Of course, if the pastor did not know the deceased, this source of information is not available. The second source is made up of stories about the deceased told by family, other grievers, and the congregation. While anticipating her death, Betty expressed her sadness at not seeing her granddaughters marry. Perhaps the dying teenager Ryan expressed his regret that he would not live out his dream to become a fireman. Perhaps the dying grandfather lamented to the pastor about his failed business and the lack of inheritance he would leave his family. In these situations of anticipated death, the pastor has heard the deceased's grief. The pastor has also listened for expressions of thankfulness and praise about the person's life, legacy, character, and contributions. The pastor has also listened for intersections of God's story with the life of the deceased. What biblical stories have come to mind as stories have been told? What has God done in and through this person's life and death? How can grievers honor this person's legacy?

• *The Stories of the Grieving.* The pastor, in listening to stories of the grieving family and others, but not only in the context of the family meeting, has heard their diverse expressions of grief. The pastor has also heard any expressions of thankfulness for their loved one and for God's care. In conversations, the pastor has listened for intersections with the grievers' stories and God's story. Where have they experienced God's loving presence or hope for new life? Or are they experiencing a sense of God's absence or powerlessness in not averting the death? Do the grievers' stories remind the pastor of biblical stories? In attending to these three dimensions of expressing grief, offering thanksgiving and praise, and proclaiming God's good news, the pastor's shaping of the funeral helps grievers with the five tasks of grieving, as the chart below indicates:

Themes in stories of deceased, grievers, congregation, and pastor	Address the five tasks of grievers:
Expressing grief	To accept the reality of death
	To express grief around the death
Offering thanksgiving and praise to God	To make meaning of the deceased's life and death
Proclaiming God's good news of loving presence and future hope	To adjust to a world in which the deceased is no longer physically present
	To redefine the relationship with the deceased in terms of memory, legacy, and love

- *The Congregation's Story.* The pastor is aware of the various effects of the death on the congregation. Assuming the deceased was an active figure in the congregation's life, the congregation must now conduct their lives without the deceased in their midst. That is, the congregation must now come to accept this person's death as a reality. Members must make meaning of it. They must envision congregational life without this person. Perhaps Mark's rich baritone voice was celebrated each week in the choir, or perhaps Ellen's daily presence brought joy and focus to the work of the food kitchen, or perhaps Jane's Sunday school teaching had been a constant for three decades. Perhaps Ethyl's death has reduced the adult Sunday school class by 33 percent. Or perhaps James was not widely loved and was a grumpy curmudgeon who was, frankly, a burr in the pastor's saddle. How will the congregation grieve what one pastor has called "a blessed subtraction"? The pastor knows of the congregation's grief or relief and of the congregation's reasons for thanks and praise. The congregational context informs the pastor's knowledge of ways that God's story has intersected with the deceased. What will God's loving presence and future hope look like for the congregation in the context of this death and the other deaths that the church has experienced?

- *The Pastor's Story.* In addition to the stories of the deceased, the grieving, and the congregation, there is also the pastor's story. How has this particular death touched the life of the pastor? Perhaps the person and the pastor had a close relationship. How does the pastor deal with his grief while also having responsibility for the funeral process? The pastor's awareness of all aspects of his or her story helps inform the ways the pastor's story will intersect with the other stories. Pastors need a deep understanding of the ways in which we can make our own wounds available as a source of healing to others, as Henri Nouwen emphasizes.[6] Remaining connected to the pain and suffering of others and ourselves while making use of our woundedness for service to others are key ingredients in effective caregiving throughout the funeral process. The pastor also knows his or her own reasons for giving thanks. The pastor may also ask what God is doing through her or him in the context of this particular death. Where is God's loving presence and hope for the pastor in these particular circumstances?

Each of these stories intersects with one another around the three elements of grief, thanksgiving, and God's good news. The pastor's attention to grief, thanksgiving and praise, and God's good news in each of the stories will inform the content of the sermon and service.

It is significant that lament psalms also intersect these same three elements. They express grief even when we cannot articulate for ourselves: "My God, my God, why have you forsaken me? Why are you so far from helping me, from the words of my groaning?" (Psalm 22:1). They offer thanksgiving and praise: "in the midst of the congregation I will praise you" (Psalm 22:22). And they proclaim God's good news: "but [God] heard when I cried to him" (Psalm 22:24).

The psalm draws these disparate elements together into a coherent process that enables grieving people as individuals and as a worship community to experience God's loving presence and future hope.

It is important to note that the three categories do not exist equally in any given funeral situation. The framing and proportion of the dimensions depend on the circumstances of the death and the needs of the grievers. The sudden death of a fourteen-year-old boy will likely foreground the experiences of grief and lament. The anticipated death of a ninety-five-year-old woman will likely foreground thanksgiving for a life well lived. But neither situation will be without the other elements.

It remains to recall what the story of God's good news looks like in the context of death and hopelessness. As outlined in chapter 1, God's story concerning how God is with God's people at times of grief has two important themes: loving presence and future hope. These two themes form a story of God's good news that is most appropriate for the funeral process. God is with God's people. God comforts God's people. God suffers with God's people. God provides hope in beckoning us into a future that offers new life. God's resurrection of Jesus demonstrates that life is greater than death and that hope has more power than despair. While these themes of presence, comfort, and hope name how God is with God's people, they also exemplify ways that we can be with one another. In the funeral, the pastor weaves God's story of loving presence and hope with the stories of the deceased, grievers, and congregation and the pastor's own story in a way that offers hope to all.

As the pastor intersects the five stories around the themes of expressing grief, offering thanksgiving and praise, and proclaiming God's good news, she or he is able to fulfill the three funeral functions:

1. *Re-presenting the deceased as a child of God.* In presenting the deceased's life and death through the filters of grief, thanksgiving and praise, and God's good news, the deceased's story is set in God's hope-bringing story.

2. *Caring for the grieving congregation.* The integration of stories around these three themes helps grievers accept the reality of death, express their grief, make meaning of the life and death, and adjust to a world in which the deceased is no longer present while redefining their relationship with the deceased in terms of memory, legacy, and love.

3. *Proclaiming God's good news.* Through words, song, prayer, and symbolic action, the funeral proclaims and manifests God's loving presence and future hope.

By weaving together all stories into the context of God's unfolding story, the pastor and family create a meaningful funeral service that re-presents the deceased, cares for the grieving congregation, and proclaims God's good news.

Conclusion

This chapter discussed the family meeting in which the pastor facilitates the tasks of grieving, gains insights and information, and makes decisions regarding the funeral service. As we turned toward the funeral service in discussing the functions of a funeral, this chapter outlined three functions for a funeral, namely, to re-present the deceased as a child of God, to care for the grieving congregation, and to proclaim God's good news. Further, I have proposed that the pastor creates a meaningful funeral by intersecting the stories of the deceased, the grievers, the congregation, and the pastor around the themes of grief, thanksgiving and praise, and the good news of God's loving presence and future hope. It is toward the task of creating the funeral service and sermon that we now turn in chapter 5.

Chapter 5

Creating the Funeral Service

In the last chapter, we saw the three functions of funerals as re-presenting the deceased as a child of God, caring for the grieving congregation through the five "tasks of grieving," and proclaiming God's good news of loving presence and future hope. It suggested that the pastor carries out these functions by weaving together the five stories of the deceased, the grievers, the congregation, the pastor, and God at their intersection points of expressing grief, offering thanksgiving, and proclaiming the good news of God's loving presence and hopeful future.

In this chapter, we discuss the creation of a meaningful funeral service that carries out these three functions informed by the intersections of the five stories. Throughout this chapter, I attend to a variety of funeral services, suggesting ways to adapt components of the funeral service to address particular circumstances. This chapter has two sections. In the first section, we discuss the art of creating a meaningful funeral service by integrating the five funeral stories through various component parts of a funeral service. In the second section, we address FAQs (Frequently Asked Questions) about funeral services and share seasoned pastors' responses to these common questions.

1. Creating a Meaningful Funeral Service

In discussing the funeral service, I use the term *funeral* to embrace both funeral and memorial services. Some appropriate elements of this service can also be selected for a committal service at a graveside, memorial garden, crematorium, or columbarium.

Here is an example of an order of service.

Sample Order of Service

- Opening Words/Invocation

- Opening Prayer

- Hymn or Song

- Words of Remembrance (reading of obituary, tributes, memories)

- Ritual That Honors the Deceased and Involves Grievers

- Reading (poem, quotation, book excerpt)

- Scripture

- Sermon

- Hymn or Song

- Prayer

- Commendation

- Holy Communion

- Prayer/Lord's Prayer

- Dismissal/Blessing

In looking at the service, how "full" will it be? The issue has to do with how many component parts will compose the order of service. A glance at several denominational books of worship indicates that their orders of worship contain more comprehensive lists than the one above, including multiple scriptural readings (Old Testament, Psalms, New Testament), prayers, creeds, and confessions of sin. Clearly there is some flexibility concerning which component parts are used and the order in which they are used. What is important is that the service re-presents the deceased as a child of God, cares for grievers, and proclaims God's loving presence and future hope.

The component parts listed above may be rearranged or omitted, which leads to a second comment. *Holy Communion* is included as a possibility. There may be contexts in which the pastor and family will choose to celebrate the Lord's Supper and other contexts in which it is not included. When the

Lord's Supper is observed, the celebration can be viewed as a farewell meal with the deceased in which the death and resurrection of Christ are made visible and present and the general resurrection anticipated, or it can be seen as a celebration of life. This ritual facilitates the grieving tasks of acknowledging and making meaning of the death. If Holy Communion is served, the family and friends of the deceased may want to bring forward the bread and wine. Given that the assembled grievers will most likely come from a variety of faith backgrounds, the pastor will want to include a warm invitation, an explanation about the meaning of Communion, and clear instructions about how Communion will be served and what worshipers are supposed to do. Still, some may choose not to partake.

Third, there is a *ritual that honors the deceased and involves grievers.* A ritual can be a personalized expression that presents the deceased's interests, passions, commitments, or activities and makes them explicit within the funeral service. For example, a funeral for a grandmother who loved gardening may include the ritual of all her grandchildren bringing forward a flower and placing it in a vase at the front of the church in honor of their grandma. In the funeral for a parishioner, Ann, who wrote poetry, the family made booklets of her unpublished poems at a local copy center and gave a copy to each funeral attendee. These rituals emerge out of the deceased's story. They involve creative symbolizing of important aspects of the deceased's identity. They provide a way for grievers to make meaning of the life and death of the deceased, a task of grieving. The ritual secures memories of the deceased for grievers in a tangible way. Important in considering a ritual is that the family sees benefit in its expression.

Fourth, the *commendation* is a prayer that asks God to receive the deceased in mercy. Similar prayers may be offered as part of the committal service at the graveside, memorial garden, crematorium, or columbarium. Even when an additional committal service precedes or follows the funeral service, it is appropriate to offer a commendation prayer in the funeral, as not everyone who attends the funeral will attend the committal service.

A fifth comment involves the component part identified as *words of remembrance.* It is common in funerals for family members and other grievers to express thoughts about the deceased. This may include reading an obituary or a poem or recalling a memory. Sometimes speakers are well prepared and focused. Others ramble at great length. Uncle Bubba may say something inappropriate. Cousin Thelma may break down and cry inconsolably. Sister Elizabeth may feel the need to make an evangelistic appeal. This raises an important question: are such speakers selected and specifically invited beforehand, or is the microphone open to anyone who wants to speak? The issue concerns balancing the need for grievers to express appropriate grief and honor for the deceased with the appropriate decorum of public worship. The pastor will need to be clear about how he or she feels about this practice in any given situation and will need to discuss this with the family. Don't be afraid to give some instruction and time limits. Some pastors, as policy, do not allow an open microphone. Other pastors think it valuable, even forty-five minutes later! Some pastors encourage or require speakers to prepare ahead of time and to create a script, even giving the pastor a copy.

The parts of the funeral service are readily identifiable. But what truly matters is the way that the pastor uses these component parts in integrating the five stories around the points of intersection identified in chapter 4, namely, expressing grief, offering thanksgiving and praise, and proclaiming God's good news of loving presence and future hope. The component parts of the service provide multiple opportunities for the pastor to articulate these points of intersection. In turn, these multiple opportunities provide grievers with numerous moments throughout the service to engage the tasks of grieving, namely, to acknowledge the death, to express grief, to make meaning of the deceased's life and death, to adjust to a world without the deceased, and to redefine the relationship with the deceased in terms of memory, legacy, and love.

First Example: Opening Words

The opening sentences of the funeral service are extremely important. They set the tone for what is to follow. A pastor who begins with, "Let not your hearts be troubled, neither let them be afraid," has immediately severed any connection with grievers in the congregation who are both troubled and afraid. Both emotions are common to grievers. Telling grievers not to be troubled and afraid does not remove these emotions. Instead, I suggest that in the opening words, the pastor connects with the grieving congregation by honestly engaging the three intersection points of expressing grief, offering thanksgiving, and proclaiming God's good news of loving presence and future hope.

Let's consider the funeral for Betty, a longtime parishioner, whose decline in health and death I described in chapter 2. To remind you, Betty died of a stroke at age eighty-two, after experiencing declining health in a nursing home for a year. Her death was anticipated.

Here are the opening words with which her pastor began her service:

> We gather together in the presence of God and one another to honor and celebrate the life of Betty Stone. We gather with mixed emotions. We are thankful for her long and rich life. We are thankful for all the ways that Betty has blessed the lives of so many, including many of us gathered here today. We are thankful for God's abiding presence with Betty as her health declined.
>
> We may also be angry at the strokes that took the Betty we knew over the last year and the stroke that finally took her life. We may be relieved that her suffering has come to an end. And we are also deeply saddened. We are sad that we no longer have Betty's physical presence—as Mother to Pam and Ben, Mother-in-Law to Bob, Grandmother to Erin and Caitlyn, aunt to Andy and Caroline, beloved teacher and friend to so many in the congregation, including myself.
>
> And so we gather and we bring all these emotions before God. We gather in the presence of God, who embraces all people in all situations. We gather to worship God.

We see in these opening words the three elements. The pastor offers thanksgiving, expresses grief, and names God's good news. Because of Betty's long life and her anticipated death, it is appropriate for the pastor to offer the three elements in similar proportion. There is much to be thankful for in Betty's life. Even though her death was anticipated, there is also much grief to name, not only at the death, but also the grief her loved ones have experienced through the many losses over the past years. There is much of God's good news to proclaim, as well. Betty was a faithful and committed member of the congregation. She encountered God's loving presence and faithfulness throughout her life. She felt God's comfort even and especially in her time of declining health, and she expressed her hope of the resurrection. This proclamation of God's good news will be well received by the congregation.

Second Example: Opening Words

We now move to a second example in a very different situation. To remind you, in chapter 3, Ellen found her twenty-one-year-old son Joe's body hanging from the rafters in the garage. Ellen speculated that Joe's drug felony, long-term unemployment, and breakup with his girlfriend led him to take his life. Though Ellen had been a church member for four years, Joe was not a member and had not attended church with his mother.

Ellen's pastor began the funeral with these opening words:

> We gather together in the presence of God and one another to honor the life of Joe Johnson. We come together, in the face of the shocking, devastating news of his suicide. We bring our questions. We bring our "what-if's." We bring our anger. We bring our regrets. We bring our deep pain and our inconsolable sorrow. We bring our deep disappointment over a bright future that is not to be. We bring our awareness of how difficult it can be to live in this world especially during times of trial. We bring our horror at the tragedy of a life ending in this way.
>
> And we bring our firm convictions that nothing—not life or death, not things present or things to come—can separate Joe or us from the love of God.
>
> We gather together with one another to give thanks for Joe's life, even though his life was cut short. We gather with Joe's mother, Ellen, his father, Eddie, and Annie and others of Joe's friends. We share your sadness and we walk with you in your pain. We gather with you. We hold you in our love and care as God holds us all in God's love and care even and especially as we walk through this valley of the shadow of devastating loss. Even and especially since, regrettably, Joe did not seem to be aware of God's sustaining love in times of trouble.

We see in these opening words the three elements. Unlike the opening words for Betty, these opening words for Joe do not contain equal representation of the three elements. Because of Joe's tragic death by suicide, greater emphasis is given to expressing myriad feelings of grief. Because of Joe's short life, less attention is given to thanksgiving. And because the pastor did not know of Joe's faith beliefs, and because the pastor knows the questions of salvation suicide evokes, God's good news here takes the form of the reassurance that nothing can separate us from God's love, even though Joe did not seem to experience it. These words let those most affected by Joe's death know that they are not alone in their devastation. The words "we hold you in our love" also appeal to the congregation as a source of love and support for Ellen and for grievers who are not church members. The assurance is given that God and the congregation are surrounding the grievers with love and care.

Third Example: Opening Words

We move now to a third example in yet another different situation. To remind you, in chapter 3, we met Carrie, a twenty-seven-year-old third-grade teacher, married to Scott, both visible and involved church members. Carrie went on a long run. Police found her abused body in a shallow grave in a nearby state park.

Here are the opening words with which Carrie's pastor began her funeral:

My God, my God, why have you forsaken me? Why are you so far from helping me, from the words of my groaning? These are the psalmist's words, and they are our words.

We have been crying out to God from the moment we learned that Carrie was missing. We cried out to God as many, many in this sanctuary searched through woods and trails and valleys and creek beds for some sign, some hope that Carrie would be found and that she would be okay.

Carrie's body was found. But our deepest hopes and our most fervent prayers were not answered. And so we say, My God, my God, why have you forsaken us? That is how it feels to Carrie's husband, Scott, to Carrie's parents, Bob and Susan, and to Scott's parents, Chris and George. That is how it feels to Carrie's church congregation—we who surrounded baby Carrie at her baptism, celebrated her confirmation, sponsored her on mission trips, and witnessed her and Scott's wedding vows almost five years ago. We feel thankful for accompanying Carrie on her deep, rich life of faith.

And we also feel deep sadness. We feel rage. We feel helpless. We feel our world is not safe. We feel devastation for Carrie's future that is no more, for the tomorrows that she and Scott will not enjoy together, for the students she will not teach, the mission trips she will no longer attend. We have no words.

Even still, as strange as it may sound, we bring our thanksgiving for the time that we did have with Carrie. We are thankful for the ways that her life touched our lives and for all the ways we are better for it. We bring all of these raw emotions to you, God. We know that though we may feel forsaken, you have not turned your back on us. You are present. Your love holds us and carries us until we can feel your comfort, your peace. As the psalmist says, "We wait for you, our Lord, our soul waits. In your word we hope. Our soul waits for the Lord more than those who watch for the morning, more than those who watch for the morning." We wait and we hope for the comfort that we will find in the Lord.

This opening statement is long. It is full and intense, voicing a range of emotional expression. The inclusion of the psalms at the beginning and the end also contributes to length. And there is the rehearsal of biographical information, which, in addition to adding to its length, also raises the question of what material might be included in the sermon.

Yet, these opening words are also doing important tasks. The pastor has a shocking and complex situation to engage. Words that name these complexities are appropriate. The opening words set the context for the entire service. The pastor's measured and appropriate tone provides comfort and reassurance to the congregation. The delivery and content allow the pastor to meet the grieving congregation where they are. We see in these opening words the three elements of grief, thanksgiving, and God's good news. Because of the tragic circumstances of murder, the pastor chooses to frame the opening words in the context of lament, using a lament psalm, Psalm 22. The words give voice to a cluster of emotions. They name the prominence of grief, but also they name thankfulness for sharing Carrie's life of faith. God's good news is given in the form of assurance of God's love and care. In the process, the words move from being an opening statement to a prayer: "We bring all these emotions to you, God." This movement from lament to prayer can be understood as being consistent with a lament psalm.

Throughout the rest of the service, these elements of grief, thanksgiving, and divine good news are elaborated in prayers, songs, readings, and sermon, and a balance of emphases unfolds. Attention is given not only to Carrie's death story but also to her life story and to the ways that God's story has been working in and through Carrie's life and death and will continue working through her legacy and in the lives of all who grieve.

Other Component Parts

In creating the funeral service, the pastor will consider which component parts to include from the possible order of service and what content each of the parts will express. These decisions will be informed by (1) the circumstances of the death and (2) the intersections of grief, thanksgiving, and God's good news that the pastor has encountered in each of the five stories of the deceased, the grieving, the congregation, the pastor, and God's story. So, in creating an appropriate and meaningful funeral service, the pastor considers questions such as:

- Given the circumstances of the life and death, what are appropriate expressions of the collected stories of grief, thanksgiving, and God's good news?

- Are there particular hymns, songs, prayers, poems, or rituals that express these three elements?

- How will these three elements of expressing grief, offering thanksgiving and praise, and proclaiming God's good news be carried out throughout the whole of the service?

First Example: Whole Service

For example, in Betty's funeral, the three elements of grief, thanksgiving, and divine good news are exemplified throughout the service in this way:

- *Opening Words:* As shown in the first example above, equal emphases are given to grief, thanksgiving, and God's good news.

- *Opening Prayer:* The pastor prays a prayer of thanksgiving for Betty's life.

- *Hymn:* "Abide with Me." This hymn celebrates God's good news of presence and comfort that Betty and her family have experienced over the past year.

- *Words of Remembrance:* Son Ben reads Betty's obituary and daughter Pam reads a tribute in which she names the family's grief, offers thanksgiving, and speaks of God's loving presence and comfort.

- *Ritual That Honors the Deceased and Involves Grievers:* Granddaughter Erin speaks about the tradition of making hard candy at Christmas. Then, Erin's sister, Caitlyn, adds that a basket of bags of homemade hard candy are at the back of the sanctuary for everyone to take as a remembrance of their grandmother's sweetness and generosity.

- *Scripture:* The pastor reads Psalm 23. Betty had shared her preference for this psalm with the pastor before she died. The psalm exemplifies God's presence, comfort, and hope.

- *Sermon:* (To be discussed in chapter 6.)

- *Hymn:* "Amazing Grace." Betty had requested and her family agreed on this hymn. Betty had felt God's graceful presence her entire life, even in her stroke-inhibited condition.

- *Prayer:* The focus of the prayer is on God's presence with grievers.

- *Commendation:* The words offer thanks to God for giving Betty to us and give Betty back to God.

- *Hymn:* "Great Is Thy Faithfulness." This hymn of thanksgiving celebrates God's faithfulness to Betty through all phases of her life and God's faithfulness to grievers throughout their grief process.

- *Dismissal/Blessing:* The pastor speaks consoling words to grievers in the context of praise to God.

Throughout the funeral service for Betty, the pastor balances the three elements of expressing grief, offering thanksgiving and praise, and proclaiming God's good news—all of which he had heard while attending to the five stories.

Second Example: Whole Service

This example takes up the service for Joe, the twenty-one-year-old suicide victim. We have already discussed the pastor's opening words. Because of Joe's age and the nature of Joe's tragic, suicidal death, the balance of the three elements of expressing grief, offering thanksgiving, and proclaiming God's good news is different from that of Betty, who died an anticipated death at a much older age. In Joe's funeral, the component parts of the service emphasize expressions of grief over offerings of thanksgiving. But thanksgiving and proclamation of God's good news are also present.

Thanksgiving for Joe's life is offered through words and song and also through visual displays. Joe was an artist. Joe's artist story is made central and visible in the funeral. Joe's oil paintings are displayed throughout the sanctuary. On a table near Joe's casket are photographs of Joe, additional paintings, and his pottery bowls, mugs, and plates. Funeral bulletins feature a reproduction of Joe's last painting, unfinished, to represent the unfinished nature of his life.

God's good news of loving presence and hope is emphasized through prayers, songs, Ellen's tribute, and the pastor's sermon. Throughout the rest of the service, the pastor integrates stories of the deceased, the grieving, the congregation, the pastor, and God's story around the points of intersection of grief, thanksgiving, and divine news in the following ways:

- *Opening Words:* As we saw in the second example on page 89, the greatest emphasis is given to expressions of grief, though thanksgiving and divine good news are also included.

- *Scripture:* At the intersection of the stories, the pastor heard from grievers who were concerned about Joe's eternal destiny. The pastor reads the following Scripture passages to reassure the grievers and to proclaim the divine good news of God's faithfulness and love in the life and death of God's children.

> If we live, we live to the Lord, and if we die, we die to the Lord; so then, whether we live or whether we die, we are the Lord's. (Romans 14:8)

> For I am convinced that neither death, nor life, nor angels, nor rulers, nor things present, nor things to come, nor powers, nor height, nor depth, nor anything else in all creation, will be able to separate us from the love of God in Christ Jesus our Lord. (Romans 8:38-39)

> In my Father's house there are many dwelling places. If it were not so, would I have told you that I go to prepare a place for you? And if I go and prepare a place for you, I will come again and will take you to myself, so that where I am, there you may be also. (John 14:2-3)

• *Opening Prayer:*

Gracious God,

We bring ourselves to you.

We bring our tears, our anger, our devastation, our questions, our pain, raw and real.

We bring our broken hearts, our broken hopes, our broken dreams.

We bring whole selves to you, O God, knowing that we are yours.

Knowing that you hold us in our brokenness.

We thank you, O God, for being with us in our deep suffering.

For surrounding us with your comfort and care even when we are too hurt to feel your comfort and care.

We do know you are with us.

And we thank you, dear God, that in Joe's life, he was yours.

And in his death, he is yours.

We thank you that there is nowhere either he or we have ever gone where you were not.

We thank you that Joe abides forever in your loving care.

Hold us in that same loving care.

We thank you for your promise that somehow, some way, we will know your peace.

Amen.

The pastor begins this prayer by expressing grievers' emotions, which she had heard in listening to their stories. The prayer transitions from grievers' pain to divine good news. Evoking Romans 14:8, the prayer reassures grievers that God welcomes all of our emotions. The prayer also reassures the congregation of God's presence with Joe in his life and death and also of God's presence with them in their grief. The prayer then moves to thanksgiving for God's continuing love and care for Joe and for the promise of God's peace.

- *Hymnn:* "Abide with Me." The hymn reinforces the good news that God abides with Joe in death as in life. God is also abiding with all grievers through the devastation of their grief.

- *Words of Remembrance:* Joe's mother, Ellen, wrote a tribute that she asked her friend from the church to read. The words speak of Joe's kind, sensitive character, his passion for painting and pottery, and his love for family, friends, and animals.

- *Scripture:* The pastor reads Romans 8:38-39: "Nothing can separate us from the love of God." The pastor emphasizes the good news of God's love in all circumstances.

- *Sermon:* (To be discussed in chapter 6.)

- *Song:* "Starry, Starry Night." Joe's family chose this song, written about artist Vincent van Gogh. Joe's story reminded Joe's family of van Gogh's story, in that both were artists and both lives were cut short. Joe's mom especially liked the words in the song, "This world was never meant for one as beautiful as you."

- *Prayer:* The focus of the prayer is on God's presence with grievers.

- *Commendation:*

Gracious God, all that you have given us is yours. You gave us Joe, and now we give him back to you. Receive Joe into the arms of your love and mercy, into the blessed rest of everlasting peace and into the glorious company of all your saints.

- *Hymn:* "O Love That Wilt Not Let Me Go." This hymn reinforces the pastor's theme of God's proactive, unconditional grace and love. Words such as, "O light that followest all my way, I yield my flickering torch to thee," affirm God's presence in Joe's and our broken lives.

- *Ritual That Honors the Deceased and Involves Grievers:* After the hymn and before the final dismissal, the pastor invites everyone to a funeral lunch immediately following the service in the church hall. She also invites everyone to participate in a ritual that recognizes and honors Joe's creative, artistic nature and contributions. The pastor explains that at lunch, there will be several canvases and art supplies on tables. All are invited to use the colored pencils, pastels, watercolor paints, or charcoals to share a memory, express a hope for the family, or draw a picture about Joe.

• *Dismissal/Blessing:*

Now, may the God of all beauty, the God who created each one of us and who continues to create all that is beautiful and loving and just and good, may this God to whose love we have entrusted Joe, may this God who comforts all who mourn offer us consoling presence, abiding comfort, and ever-present hope in the name of the Father, the Son, and the Holy Spirit now and forever. Amen.

We see in the above order of service that thanks are given for Joe's life, even though it was tragically cut short. God's good news—in the form of God's creative activity, grace, love, and care—is affirmed. This order of service demonstrates ways in which the pastor can thoughtfully and carefully balance the elements of expressing grief, offering praise and thanksgiving, and proclaiming God's good news in ways that are appropriate to the situation.

Each pastor will have his or her own way of appropriately balancing these three elements throughout the funeral service. What I have attempted to demonstrate in this section is that a meaningful and faithful funeral service will include these elements at the intersection points of the five stories that compose the funeral process.

2. FAQs about Funeral Services

As pastors create funeral services, there are common questions that arise. In this section, I identify some frequently asked questions. I catalog some responses solicited from seasoned pastors.[1]

• What is your advice for ways that pastors can best help families in the funeral process?

    o There are two essential pastoral functions around funeral/ memorial services. The one we think of is the service itself. The other essential function is the family meeting that takes place, ideally, several days beforehand. This meeting has an overt goal of planning the service to align with the wishes of family. The deeper function is to provide an avenue for the loved ones present to share their stories about the life of the one who passed. Telling stories is very important, and in our culture we don't have lots of outlets for this. (Where is the Irish wake when you need it?) Frequently, the family needs to "out" some bit of awkwardness or fear. Examples include: the deceased was an alcoholic who frequently hurt people emotionally and physically; some family members are estranged; some family members are already circling for the "stuff"; the deceased wasn't always a good mom; the youngest son is gay.

o Be prepared when you talk to the family. Have questions handy that might elicit some good stories about the authentic person, not about the false mask he or she wore. *What surprised you about Mary? Tell me about some crossroads that Jim faced and the direction he ultimately chose. What did he think was funny about life and people? What was she afraid of? What was the moment of greatest courage in her life? Tell me about Mary's legacy to you, in terms of her influence in forming who you are.*

o I am amazed at how often the family needs to get something said—something weighing heavy on their minds. When a pastor listens openly and nonjudgmentally these things usually come bursting forth. Telling the life stories and the family's complicated stories is hugely important to the healing process of the families.

o Listening to the family and close friends is key. Allow your presence/attitude to be consistent with theirs, while bringing a sense of hope and promise and dignity. The behavior of family and friends during "visitation" can be informative. For some, a smile and even laughter is imperative.

o It is normal and natural for families to experience conflict in the funeral process. Family members may try to dominate the conversation, insisting that their version of events surrounding the death or that their preferences are the "correct" ones. As a facilitator of a family conversation, a pastor can help by assuring that each person experiences events and relationships uniquely. She can remind the family that it is important for the family to hear each other's stories, experiences, and preferences. When preferences around funeral decision making differ, often the pastor and funeral director can help the family consider different perspectives.

o It can be important to focus on the circumstance of the death early on and not the relationships with the deceased. Survivors need to tell you the entire story as they see it. You only have to ask what happened, and the family will tell you. But the emphasis here is not on getting the facts straight, but on helping the family.

o The family's humorous stories about the deceased can be helpful and healing, if they are shared without malice. Some family members may dump a gunnysack of bad feelings they are carrying from the past.

o Pay close attention to all logistical details, and be certain that the family knows what to expect.

o I usually ask if there are particular topics that should be avoided; often there is a sensitive area that should not be brought to attention. I always ask what will be missed if it is not said during the service.

o It's important to involve families in the planning of the service. As a pastor, I'm not there to force my agenda on them. I often ask about the deceased's favorite hymn, song, poem, passage of Scripture or Bible story, and so on.

o A celebration of life should focus on the whole of life and not dwell on the most recent (sometimes most difficult) days to the exclusion of earlier times. I always ask about an adult's childhood, shaping influences, other churches that were meaningful, and so on.

• What have you learned over the years by doing funerals?

o I remember doing my first funeral and thinking that it is impossible to sum up someone's life in a few minutes and a few words. It is impossible, but I learned very early that it is possible to capture someone's life in a few minutes. If I just get out of the way, the spirit of the person will be present, not in a "spooky" way, but in the memories and lived experiences of those who have come to the funeral. The pastoral (p)art is weaving the scripture story into the story of the deceased's life.

- What does the pastor do when the deceased was a difficult person?
  - o I try to find a way to tell the truth in the service. If a person was a colossal jerk, I don't say that per se, but I'm not going to say, "Joe was a saint on this earth," either. In one case, I said, "John was a complicated man and not always an easy one." And the main thrust of the sermon was for the family to use this as an opportunity for second chances, new beginnings. This is part of honoring the story. I look hard to find redemption. I preach redemption, even if it isn't always of the deceased person.
  - o It can be a difficult task, at times, to keep the funeral a worship service in which the worship is of God and not the deceased person. Family and friends who want to speak will want to focus almost solely on the exploits of the person in the casket. I've even heard flat lies that I knew were lies and that even children in the congregation knew were lies, told either about the deceased or about the relationship between the speaker and the deceased. Our job is to complete a gentle dance between reminding folk of their loved one and reminding folk of the love of God that sustains no matter what. That means telling the truth, without being brutal, about how Uncle Joe was a sinner like us but that God's grace was seen at least somewhere in his life. I've done funerals for saints and suicides, for one serial killer, and for children too young or disabled ever to "do" anything worthy of the newspapers. In the most faithful worker there were mistakes and limitations and sin. In the worst actors there was the possibility being offered for something better. In the youngest and least able there is a witness to the sheer grace that saves without any counting of good works. Our job is honesty, but honesty tempered with respect, grace, and mercy.

- What about secular music in a funeral service?
  - o In our church, we allow secular music. Hymns are lovely and often comforting, but sometimes a family wants to

hear "Desperado" more than "How Great Thou Art." Secular music is particularly helpful during a slide show of the person's life. There is so much emotional content to music! It is a pastoral act to allow it. I even had an organist once tell me that a family requested the song "I Won't Miss You."

- Any advice about doing a funeral for someone the pastor doesn't know?

    o If you were not acquainted with the deceased, you do not need to call attention to that fact. Those for whom that information is pertinent (close family) will already be aware of that fact and may feel unnecessarily guilty about that reality. Without perjuring one's self, it is simple to use phrases such as, "I understand he/she . . ." or, "It has been said that . . ." or even, "You knew her/him as . . ."

- How long is a typical service?

    o Few services need to be longer than forty-five minutes, and most can be appropriately complete at thirty-five to forty minutes or even less, depending on the music.

- What about family and friends who want to speak at the service?

    o Respect the right of close family members to have input. Encourage them to put thoughts in writing, which you may quote or summarize in appropriate ways. If they are to speak, encourage them to "overly prepare" and use a script and to keep remarks appropriately brief at five minutes.

    o Manage any spoken input from others (eulogies, etc.). Do not take for granted that everyone who wishes to speak should be allowed to do so; it is the family's preference that matters, along with your input. In your sanctuary/church, the final call is yours, not necessarily that of the family friend. You do not have to allow a third party to preach a message that is inconsistent with your church's tradition.

- What about funeral attendees who do not regularly attend church?

    o For some of these attending, this will be a rare occasion of being "in church." They may need to be reassured that the service will be welcoming, not judging. Remember that most of those attending did not come to hear you or expect to be uplifted but are there simply to honor the deceased and his or her family. Noting your own personal experiences with the deceased may or may not be helpful to the process.

o In some traditions, the service is an opportunity to "save" someone, but whatever your view, it is not meant to be a time to correct the theological point of view of those attending.

• What about using poetry in a service?

o Poetry should not become a substitute for your own words and thoughts. People generally prefer simple honesty and the speaker's own words.

• Any thoughts about working with funeral directors?

o I have found that funeral home directors are great at *directing*. Young pastors can likely rely on them to be quite helpful.

• What about if I cry in the pulpit?

o It's okay to get misty-eyed as you speak. Don't break down, but it's okay to show some feeling.

o You need to be emotionally empathic in leading the worship, but your emotions need to be under control. Use visualization to prepare for the occasion. Attend funeral services and put yourself in the place of the person leading. How do you manage a funeral preparation in the midst of an already full week?

o As you prepare, if you think that you will be too emotional to conduct the service, ask another pastor either to help or to lead the service entirely after informing the family. The pastor should not be a distraction during the service, and if you think that you might be one, it is better to step aside.

• What do you think about the common habit of speaking in the name of the deceased?

o Thou shalt not ever, ever, ever place your own words in the mouth of the deceased! It is unprofessional and often hurtful for the family. For example, do not say, "I know Aunt Sue would want everyone here to accept Jesus before they leave today," or—this from the funeral of a two-year-old who was likely the victim of child abuse—"Ron would want you to know that he fought the good fight and has finished the race." Remarks like these are presumptuous.

- What about military involvement in funerals?
  - o When an active duty member or an immediate family member is killed, a Casualty Assistance Calls Officer (CACO) is available to assist the family throughout the funeral process. Pastors and military representatives work together to create a funeral that represents the family's wishes, is consistent with military protocol, and carries out the pastor's functions of the funeral. Military ceremonies have standard service elements that seek to provide the highest level of honors to the family. When a pastor dishonors service elements, it is seen as a dishonor to the military service, to the service member, and to the family. A pastor uses sensitivity in negotiating these tensions while being faithful to the Christian tradition.

- Any last words on funerals?
  - o I have never used a funeral as an occasion to generate an "altar call," however, some people come to a funeral ready to hear whether God has anything to say about death and life—the deceased's and our own. So I preach the gospel and try to say, "Yes, God has something to say."
  - o The work of preparing for grief is a part of every sermon we preach. Honesty cannot begin at the deathbed. With church-attending folk, one must have already and consistently acknowledged that not every scripture is helpful or true at every moment. They are sometimes the very reason that people have a hard time. Rejoice always and the biblical passages that refer to David's son dying as punishment for David's sin with Bathsheba immediately come to mind.
  - o Funerals are hard. But they're also opportunities for the most beautiful expressions of our faith. If you want to affect the faith of your community, and if you want to bring God's good word to a hurting world, you will plan out funeral services with care and love.
  - o Although it may be tempting, do not repeat funeral messages. In my experience there will always be someone who

will know, and it says that you didn't really care about doing something special just for the deceased.

Over time, every pastor accumulates wisdom and preferences around funeral services, while also realizing that each funeral service is different because each situation is different.

Chapter 6

Creating the Funeral Sermon

The previous chapter discussed ways to create a meaningful funeral service that re-presents the deceased as a child of God, cares for the grieving congregation, and proclaims God's good news of God's loving presence and future hope. Through the component parts of the service, the pastor expresses grief, thanksgiving and praise, and God's good news. Throughout this chapter, we'll discuss the funeral sermon, suggesting ways that the sermon contributes to these same purposes.

This chapter has two sections. In section 1, I discuss the functions of funeral sermons. In section 3, there are excerpts from funeral sermons that carry out these functions.

1. Functions of Funeral Sermons

Just as there are differing perspectives on the functions of funerals, there are also differing perspectives on the functions of funeral sermons. On one end of the spectrum are those, such as Thomas Long and William Willimon, who assert that the main purpose of a funeral sermon is proclaiming hope in Christ.[1] At the other end of the spectrum are secular eulogies that celebrate a life. These sermons give numerous details of a person's family, accomplishments, career, and hobbies, with little or no acknowledgment of God.

I am among those in the middle of the spectrum who suggest that the funeral sermon serves multiple functions.[2] I propose that the funeral sermon, as with the rest of the funeral service, functions to re-present the deceased as a child of God, care for the assembled grievers in their tasks of grieving, and proclaim the good news of God's loving presence and future hope. Naming this good news is important. But the good news is not asserted without context. Rather, God's good news is affirmed in the context of the deceased's particular life and death, surrounded by these particular grievers, being addressed by this particular pastor.

How does the pastor re-present the deceased as a child of God, care for the assembled grievers, and proclaim God's good news in the funeral sermon? Chapters 4 and 5 suggested that the pastor carries out these functions in creating the funeral service by intersecting the five stories of the deceased, the grievers, the congregation, the pastor, and God at their intersection points of expressing grief, offering thanksgiving, and proclaiming God's good news. This same approach also applies to the funeral sermon; though in the sermon, greater emphasis is given to expressing grief and proclaiming God's good news. Thanksgiving to God for aspects of the person's life and death is much more often offered in prayers and songs throughout the service.

In creating the funeral sermon, the pastor integrates these five stories around the intersecting points of expressing grief and proclaiming the good news of God's loving presence and future hope. The pastor can integrate the stories by using a three-part rubric comprising:

1. The person's life story.

2. The person's death story.

3. God's story as revealed in the person's life and death.

Each of these component parts is important. The content of each is significant for integrating the five stories. Depending on the life and death circumstances, these component parts can be utilized in different ways. They can be integrated, rearranged, or one can be fore-grounded while another is receded. Each part is presented in the context of the other two parts. The person's life is presented in the context of the person's death. The person's death is presented in the context of the person's life. The person's life and death are presented in the context of God's story as revealed in the person's life and death.

2. Funeral Sermon Examples

Elaborating on these three component parts, here are some examples.[3]

Intersections between the Person's Life Story and God's Story

What should the pastor choose to say about the person's life story? Unlike the sermon in a secular funeral, the focus of the life story is not merely a catalog list of family members, jobs, accomplishments, hobbies, and places lived. It is not a function of the Christian funeral to glorify or worship the deceased. One of the funeral's functions is to re-present the deceased as a child of God who is returning to God's eternal presence. Hence, in the sermon, the pastor re-presents intersections of the person's life story with the assembled grievers' stories and with God's story.

The pastor is able to do so because, in hearing stories about the deceased prior to the funeral service, the pastor has been discerning: What about the deceased's life is being grieved? How have we seen God's story unfold in this person's life? Where are we seeing God's loving presence and future hope?

The pastor's presentation of the life story in the sermon makes particular what is lost with the person's death, helping the assembled grievers recall and grieve particular traits about or experiences with the deceased. It helps reinforce or reinterpret memories of the deceased, especially when these memories are set in the context of God's gracious, hopeful story. Such memory making is one of the tasks of grieving. Pastors portray these intersections among the person's life story, grievers' stories, and God's story in various ways.

Lynn's Death

Pastor Jeff evokes a biblical scene. In his sermon for Lynn, a longtime, faithful church member, he speaks of her love for gardening. After quoting Genesis 2:8-9, which begins, "The LORD God planted a garden in Eden," he says:

> Everywhere Lynn Waters ever lived, she planted a garden. No matter what, she said, we have to have a garden. In the end, gardening was not about success to Lynn. It was the garden itself that mattered; it was a little bit of Eden for Lynn's home.

The pastor concludes the sermon with:

> This day Lynn walks in God's beautiful garden. For her there is reunion. And for us, in God's good time, there will be reunion as well. Until then, let us live in the joy and gratitude and celebration and love for the fullness of God's gift of life that Lynn shared with all of us.

Notice how the pastor picks up one of Lynn's hobbies—gardening—and sets it in the context of the story of Eden, thereby affirming God's presence with Lynn throughout her life. He intersects the gardening story with the good news of resurrection hope for all.

Carl's Death

Analogous biblical characters provide another way of intersecting a life story, grievers' stories, and God's story. Pastors might link the deceased with any one of numerous biblical characters: Martha's serving heart, Paul's fervor, Priscilla's leadership, or the prodigal's repentance. Pastor Katie led the funeral for Carl, a regular worship attendee. In his eighties, he confessed to the pastor that he had "seen too much [to] believe all that stuff about God—hook, line, and sinker." But when he became ill with congestive heart failure, he wondered with her, "whether God could receive someone like me." In the funeral sermon, Pastor Katie names Carl's struggle to believe. She connects the scene involving the father of the sick child who cries out to Jesus, "I believe! Help my unbelief!" (Mark 9:14-29) with Carl's situation:

> One day in the hospital, a couple of weeks ago, the conversation came around again to the promises of God, that God never lets us go, that God was holding Carl in God's hands right at that very moment. Carl looked at me with his blue eyes open wide and said, "I think I believe that. I haven't always known for sure, but I think now I do."

> "I think now I do." "I believe; help my unbelief." Five words. Not an earth-shattering confession of unwavering faith, but a naked confession of the true nature of Carl's heart, his yearning for God's promises and power, his acknowledgment of need, his call for God's help. The prayer of a man who doesn't know what else to say, who offers up his imperfect faith in exchange for God's power, hoping beyond hope for the only help in the universe that can make one bit of difference now.

Having described Carl entrusting himself to God's gracious power, she moves on to the gathered grievers:

> "I believe; help my unbelief." It has always been in God's nature to take the shreds of our faith—the precious shreds, all the scraps of our humanity we manage to hang on to as we sojourn through this life—to take those scraps and shreds and

tangled knots of confusion and weave them into the rightly colored tapestry of all the saints, all the conflicted, struggling believers who came before us, all the conflicted, struggling believers who follow after us. Carl is woven into the tapestry of saints now—Carl and his confession, Carl and his faithful, conflicted, truthful prayer.

Pastor Katie connects Carl, the grievers, and the communion of saints. She continues by linking all of them with resurrection hope:

And now Carl knows for sure what we are still hoping to see with clarity, someday. His unbelief is no more. Belief is all that's left, pure and uncompromised, and with it comes the lifting up, the hand of Jesus lifting up the one assumed dead, the raising up to health and strength and joy—all the promises of life with God fulfilled, completely, unambiguously, for Carl Adams, and eventually for us, too.

Tim's Death

Pastor Holly uses the parishioner's middle name to evoke a biblical character. After describing Tim's upbringing and relationships, she says:

His family always called him Stephen, his middle name. In many ways that was a good fit. Stephen was the early church founder who was put in charge of caring for the poor, organizing the disciples. He did that. But everywhere he went, he talked about his faith boldly, honestly. If folks were stiff-necked, ornery, or out of line, he told them to straighten up and that they needed to change. That was Tim Stephen Conner. He told the truth.

The pastor, in aligning Tim's story with Stephen's, casts gospel light on Tim's truth telling.

Joan's Death

Whereas pastors Katie and Holly evoke biblical characters, Pastor Tom picks up a theme that recurs throughout Scripture. He uses the theme of "storms" to connect the life story of a woman who died in her 70s after a struggle with Alzheimer's disease. The pastor did not know Joan, though her brother, John, was a parishioner. At the beginning of his sermon, Pastor Tom reports on a conversation he had with John about Joan. The storm image emerged from this conversation:

> I asked, "Was she an anxious person?" To which John replied, "No, but she didn't like storms!" No, she did not like storms. Storms are a part of the created world and order. Storms reshape the landscapes of our communities and our very lives. And to this we might all agree: the illness that overtook Joan came like a storm, and neither she nor we have to like it."

Having connected Joan's dislike of storms and the storm of her illness, the pastor evokes Psalm 46:1-3: "God is our refuge and strength, a very present help in trouble. Therefore we will not fear, though the earth should change, though the mountains shake in the heart of the sea; though its waters roar and foam, though the mountains tremble with its tumult." He speaks of Joan's family—the ways that she cared for them and how, during the storm that shook and overwhelmed her life, they cared for her. He then exhorts the assembled grievers to be proactive in finding ways through the inevitable storms of their lives, knowing that God's love is found in and through loving family relationships:

> Especially in storms that linger, take shelter in what we know and trust, and continue to cling to and trust in God. Cherish your family and your extended family; they are part of God's way of meeting your needs today and tomorrow and beyond.

The pastor then speaks resurrection hope for Joan and the assembled grievers, inviting them to celebrate their positive memories of Joan:

> The season of this storm in Joan's life has passed. She has stepped once again into the light of God's peaceful presence. And after the storm of these recent months and this week, the sky will once again smell fresh and the breeze will again be gentle and the brilliance will again remind us of the light that shines through the darkness in God's son who brings grace. What are the joyful memories that Joan has given you? Gifts of laughter and affection? These deepest memories will become even more sharply defined once the story of the moment has passed. You may always remember the grief. But speak of the laughter and the healing and the comfort. And we will remember, as Joan has been brought to remember with certainty, the eternal love that embraces and enfolds, bringing wholeness again to that which was once threatened by the storms and broken by the winds.

By entwining Joan's story and the grievers' stories in the context of God's eternal story, the pastor assures those gathered that their sorrow, though significant, is not ultimate. The pastor helps them make meaning out of Joan's life, disease, and death and facilitates the formation of a new relationship with Joan—one of memory, love, and spirit.

Ed's Death

Sometimes meaningful intersections among a person's life story, grievers' stories, and God's story are difficult to identify. Pastor Katherine knew Ed to be a tough old man before he died in his 90s. The pastor's meetings with family confirmed her experiences of Ed and her impression that he was a mean man whom no one liked—not even his second wife and adult sons. The congregation's memory of Ed was that he attended church only to vote against issues.

In preparing the sermon, the pastor took these stories and recast them by introducing the idea of God at work in Ed's life in perhaps very hidden and surprising ways, despite all appearances to the contrary. In her sermon, after elaborating the theme of Ed "working hard and playing hard," the pastor paints a picture of a possible intersection of Ed's story and God's story:

> I was surprised to hear that in Montana, where he and Bev and the family would spend summers, Ed would leave the house every day and find himself a place by the river. He'd sit there by himself all day, watching the river. What a picture. As I thought about it, it came to me—that's a beautiful image of prayer. Ed would probably laugh if he ever heard me say that. But that kind of solitude—just in and of itself—is an invitation to the Divine. That kind of solitude has a way of tearing a little hole in the fabric of "normal" space and time such that the Eternal can make an appearance. In solitude, God can manifest simply as a sense of peace or a sense of wonder at creation or a new appreciation of beauty or a long-lost memory that pops up and brings a little chuckle or a tear.

Pastor Katherine, in describing Ed's times at the river, presents this possibility of God's mystery intersecting with Ed's story. In doing so, the pastor offers grievers the opportunity for a new relationship with Ed after his death. By reframing and reinterpreting a surprising memory in a surprising way, the pastor opens the door to fresh or reinterpreted memories of Ed.

Mark's Death

In a funeral sermon for twenty-seven-year-old Mark Jensen, Pastor Jeff exhibits another approach to the intersection of stories. He draws on the biblical focus on new life and somatic transformation (1 Corinthians 15) with the image of a cocoon and a butterfly. Mark, severely handicapped from a birth injury, regularly attended worship with his family. Confined to a wheelchair, he did not speak. Mark's dad preceded him in death by a few years. The pastor begins his sermon by interweaving Mark's story with those of his family and caregivers and by setting all in the context of God's presence, love, and provision.

> Mark Jensen lived a miraculous and grace-filled life. The miracles and the grace Mark experienced came to him from God and from those whom God had given to Mark as a gift in his life—his family, Rob and Toni, Rich, and Carl; and two wonderful and dedicated caregivers, Emily and Jill. These folk brought love, compassion, and constancy into Mark's life in a way that teaches us something about the boundless love of God. Because of them and because of God's constant presence, in spite of the severity of his physical disabilities, Mark's life was filled with miracles and grace.

The pastor then introduces the cocoon theme that he will use throughout the sermon. The cocoon becomes a metaphor, not only for Mark's condition, but also for sacred places of connection with Mark:

> Mark's father used to say that Mark was in a cocoon. The cocoon was impenetrable for many people. But for those who chose to be patient and to wait, the mysterious life of the Spirit was revealed in their relationships with Mark. There were the responses that were neither predictable nor regular, but they were there day by day—the smiles, the reactions to different kinds of stimuli, the tear rolling down his face at a particularly poignant moment at his dad's memorial service.

Pastor Jeff then names intersections between the congregation and Mark. First, he explains a meaningful ritual in place for the funeral:

> We are wearing our red stoles today instead of the traditional white in honor of Mark because it seemed as if Mark could see and respond to red in a special way. For his family, his caregivers, and friends who waited, Mark offered an intimate if mysterious look inside his cocoon.

Later in the sermon, the pastor connects Mark's life and death story to God's story of resurrection hope. He invites the assembled grievers to picture scenes of physical wholeness and shared activity:

> Inside a cocoon is a life that is waiting to emerge as a butterfly. The images that emerge for those who love Mark have been numerous and varied—the sight of an empty wheelchair with the merest whisper of a shadow as Mark walks away; Mark and his father, Rob, throwing a football to each other in some field of dreams in heaven, walking away from their game hand in hand; imagined conversations that would build upon the mysterious communion of this life; Toni finding the spiritual strength to lift Mark up to God and the communion of saints and Rob reaching down to take him to his new home. The cocoon is broken open. The butterfly has emerged.

He concludes by including the assembled grievers in God's story of hope and promise:

> Sisters and brothers, let us rejoice that Mark is free—the butterfly has emerged—to run and dance and sing beside his dad in the heavenly choir and talk and shout. Let us rejoice in the reunion that is his. And let us hope for the reunion that will be ours.

Throughout his sermon, Pastor Jeff brings the assembled grievers into Mark's cocoon. By using the cocoon and butterfly image, he not only describes Mark's transformation but also helps the assembled grievers transform the ways that they think about Mark—through the lens of miracle, grace, and love.

Joe's Death

Pastor Ginger takes a different approach. She evokes a novel, *The Life of Pi*, to show connections between God's story and Joe's life. Joe is the father of her neighbor, Rob. Joe died at age sixty-three after many years of hard living. Neither Joe nor Rob went to church. Though estranged for years, they had recently reconnected.

Pastor Ginger begins her sermon:

> In Yann Martel's novel *Life of Pi*, the main character tells an amazing story of being on a life raft with a Bengal tiger for 227 days after a shipwreck. As Pi tells his story, it becomes apparent

that it might not be factually true. "So tell me, since it makes no factual difference to you and you can't prove the question either way, which story do you prefer? Which is the better story, the story with animals or the story without animals?" Which is the better story? That seems to me to be a theme in Joe Anderson's life.

The pastor goes on to name, honestly, truths about Joe's life—that he was known to tell his own tall tales, that he abandoned his two children, Kerry and Rob, at young ages, that he abused alcohol and drugs, and that eventually he cleaned up his life. Through a series of coincidences, which the pastor attributes to the Holy Spirit, he reconnected with Kerry and Rob. Having named the Divine story at the intersection of Joe's and Kerry and Rob's stories, the pastor continues:

> Kerry and Rob, in hearing a bit of your stories, I want you to know how inspired I am by both of you. You could easily have adopted victim stories about your childhoods without your dad. But far from it. You have both found a way to tell the story that lets his role in your lives—even when he wasn't physically present—be a source of strength. You have chosen the better story. Instead of bitterness, you have chosen gratitude.

And she names Joe's story as one of redemption:

> Joe's life teaches us something that Jesus' life also shows: everything will be all right in the end. If it's not all right, it's not the end. It is perfectly clear to me that Joe is now home with the Creator, healed and whole. Because this isn't all there is. Ultimately that is the better story.

The pastor proclaims the good news that God's story of redemption and hope is the ultimate story—into which all stories are embraced.

One of the component parts of the funeral sermon composes, then, representing the person's life story as a child of God, one whose life story intersected with grievers' stories and God's story. A second component part of the funeral sermon involves naming the person's death story.

Intersections between the Person's Death Story and God's Story

The role that the death story has in the sermon is determined by the way a person died. If the deceased had a long, satisfying life and died an anticipated death in old age and in circumstances well known to many, the death story may not need much prominence. However, if the death was unexpected, protracted, or tragic, such as a stillbirth, car accident, medical complication, devastating disease, or suicide, the manner of death undoubtedly will be weighing heavily on the minds and hearts of those present. As the pastor chooses what to emphasize about the death story, she considers: What will help the assembled grievers make sense of this death? How have God's presence, comfort, and hope been manifested through the person's death and surrounding events?

Naming the death story is important, particularly in circumstances that some might regard as shameful. Sensitively naming the circumstances of death helps grievers acknowledge and accept the death while also setting the context for subsequent support for grievers. The way the pastor presents the death helps grievers make meaning of it. Yet, the pastor will also want to acknowledge that the death story is not ultimate, that it does not eclipse the life story, and that all stories are part of God's gracious, eternal story.

John's Death

John Manning was a twenty-three-year-old college athlete who died unexpectedly in his sleep. Pastor Meg begins her sermon by clearly naming the shock and suddenness of John's death. Recalling a conversation with John's mom, Leslie, she says:

> Leslie, you told me that John came fast into this world on that first day of November just twenty-three years ago. John came into this world fast. We're here today because John left this world fast. Too fast. Many of you gathered here are John's peers: his classmates, teammates, cousins, friends. Like my own, your young hearts may be asking why. Why John? Why so fast? Why so young?

She affirms the apparent senselessness and unfairness of John's death:

> The truth is that there is no explanation that makes this okay. Friends, your anger and questions are fair. John's death is not fair. There is nothing okay about this. It was too fast.

Subsequently, without attempting to "explain" his death or to defend God, she locates their grief within the loving presence of God:

> We don't know the answers to why; but we do know, we can know, and today we will say out loud that John is okay. John

is okay because death—no matter how fast, no matter how tragic—has no power to pull us away from God. John is okay because God raised our Lord Jesus from the dead and in his resurrection is the promise of our own. John belongs to God, and nothing can separate John or us from God's love.

After locating John in God's love and resurrecting power, the pastor emphasizes God's love and care for the assembled grievers:

In life and in death John belonged to God, as do we all. And even today God is here saying to our grieving hearts: I am with you. Do not fear. When you pass through the waters, I will be with you; and through the rivers, they shall not overwhelm you. My friends, the waters through which you will pass in these days ahead—the deep and dark waters of grief—will certainly feel overwhelming. The waters of grief come in waves, and they knock the very breath out of us. The promise is that God will be there through the waters—in the waters—and indeed, I believe that parts of those waters are the very tears of God. They are tears shed for John, tears of love, and tears over one beloved child gone too fast.

Without ever attempting to justify John's death, the pastor reassures grievers that God, who suffers with them, will sustain them in the devastation of their grief.

Steve's Death

A funeral sermon for fifty-four-year-old Steve presented different challenges. Steve died from alcoholism. Pastor George chooses to begin by naming mostly positive memories gathered in conversations with the family:

There is so much about Steve that needs to be remembered. Linda, his mother, remembers a happy, blue-eyed, blond-haired boy, inquisitive and smart, who became a young man while attending First Church, who was active with the youth group, and who fell in love with Mary and called her "my lady." John, his dad, remembers how much his family meant to him, hanging the family tree his brother Chris framed in the center of his place to see it every day. Aaron, his son, remembers the trips to the cabin where his dad taught him and Christa to fish.

The pastor then names the addiction that killed Steve:

But there are some things in Steve's life that must also be remembered. Steve had a life-long struggle with addiction to alcohol. He tried so many times to overcome it. Rehab, twelve-step programs—he had done it all, more than once, yet he'd succumb to the disease of alcohol again. It broke his marriage. Although he wasn't abusive to his kids, because of him, life for them was more of a struggle. They are grateful for the times he was there, but clearly there were many times he simply wasn't present. It led to his untimely and tragic death at fifty-four.

The pastor then sets these life and death stories in the context of God's story:

It is not easy to name these things. But John 8:32 says, "The truth will make you free." Today in the holiness of this sanctuary, we need to face all the truth and find the freedom that Steve would hope we would find today. For finally there is something more we need to remember today. Psalm 23 has this line: "Even though I walk through the darkest valley..." Steve walked in that valley. Addiction is like walking alone in darkness. We really don't want to go the way the trail is taking us, but it seems beyond our choice.

The pastor connects Steve's story of addiction with the assembled grievers:

There are events like that in all of our lives. Maybe we are at war and decisions seem to thrust themselves on us. Maybe a decision has to be made by a patient's bed or a choice has to be made about a marriage, or a thousand other choices need to be made along the way.

He continues, using his own story, by testifying to God's resurrecting power:

I am an adult child of alcoholic parents. My dad died when I was twenty-five, his life cut short by cirrhosis of the liver. My mom died when I was in my forties. In the arms of Jesus, my mother is now her full self. In Jesus, the perishable has been transformed to the imperishable. And so it is with Steve. Steve is now transformed to what he could not become in his own power. He is free, whole, healthy. Today we celebrate not only what is worth remembering about Steve but also what is true of our faith.

With these words, Pastor George connects Steve and the assembled grievers with his own story and with an experience of God's resurrecting power.

Norman's Death

The death story for Norman, an eighty-year-old retired doctor, was all-consuming for his church congregation. On a trip to Israel, Norman had disappeared from his tour group. There was much prayer. The search for him included local and national authorities. There was national media attention. Four days later, his body was discovered. He had died of dehydration and exposure.

Pastor Jim begins his sermon by naming the congregation's experience of God's apparent failure to answer their fervent prayers:

> This is not what we prayed for. Whenever we first heard of Norman's disappearance and began to pray, this is not what you or I hoped for or prayed for. We had prayed that maybe it was a simple mistake of getting on a wrong bus.

After naming the challenge of accepting the reality of Norman's death, the pastor evokes the ascent to the temple in Psalm 121. He describes the difficulty of and risk in the journey up the mountain to Jerusalem. He then connects the psalm's content to Norman's story:

> Psalm 121 does not promise that the journey will be easy or that we will all make it to Jerusalem, but Psalm 121 promises that God will be with us all along the way wherever we go. Psalm 121 is a song of hope for the journey—the journey of our lives, but also the journey of faith. Norman was a lifelong pilgrim on the journey of faith. However he met his end, he was not alone, because God was traveling with him. When he took his last breath in this world, he took his first breath in the next. My deepest prayer for Norman and for you and me is that whenever the journey brings detours, roadblocks, or even abrupt ends, God is with us.

With these words, the pastor provides assurance about God's presence with Norman in life, death, and beyond, and with the assembled grievers.

Another pastor, Pastor Mike, also spoke at the same funeral for Norman. He was with Norman and his wife, Ann, on the trip. For four days, while they searched desperately for Norman, Mike accompanied Ann. He concludes with these words that also incorporate the journey theme appropriate to Norman's death while traveling to the Holy Land:

> More than once during those four days when Norm was missing, Ann commented about the look on his face when he walked off in Beth Shean. She said she had never seen a look like that on his face. It was a look of determination, like he was heading somewhere on purpose. Of course, now we know where he was going. He was crossing the river. He was going to see God. It was his trip to the Holy Land.

Pastor Mike also provides reassurance that Norman is in the presence of God, thereby helping the assembled grievers both accept and make meaning of Norman's death.

Dale's Death

In a particularly difficult situation, Dale, a twenty-nine-year-old man, killed his wife and sixteen-month-old daughter before committing suicide. His mother asked Elder Linda to lead his funeral service. She begins her sermon by naming the tragic circumstances:

> Over a week ago, unspeakable tragedy befell this family, and three lives were lost. It's the kind of devastating news that no parent, no sibling, no friend should ever have to hear. It's too awful for words. There is pain among us that the best of human medicine cannot cure. But for Christians, there is a balm that can ease the pain. We call for that healing touch now.

After the choir sings "There Is a Balm in Gilead," Linda names the ever-present, unanswerable questions:

> We all ask, "How can this happen?" and "Why, God? O why?" And the response is, "We don't know. We cannot know. We may never know." But I'd like to remind you, Terri, Robert, Scott, and all your family and friends, of some things that we *do* know.

Linda goes on to affirm aspects of Dale's life story. She provides assurance that nothing—not even these dreadful circumstances—can separate people from the love of God. She affirms God's care for the grieving family, expressed through friends, relatives, and congregation members. The murder and suicide, though incomprehensibly tragic, are not ultimate in the love of God.

Lou's Death

After consulting with Lou's wife, Rabbi Jonathan sensitively identifies Lou's death as a suicide. He begins his sermon:

> We grieve Lou's untimely and tragic death, together with his wife, Sharon, and his children [and other relatives]. I have spoken with Sharon, and we have agreed that it need not be a secret that Lou died by his own hand. It is high time for us to move beyond the stigma and shame of suicide. Those of us who have known or witnessed the bleakness of suicidal depression and have escaped its clutches know that in the depths of depression's grip, there is no hope; death appears better than continued living. It is tragic, but it should no longer be a hushed and stigmatized affair when a suicide occurs. Empathy is called for. We are called to compassion, not to harsh judgment, to sorrow, not to accusation, as we consider the desperation that makes one's death appear to be the only path to peace and wholeness.

Rabbi Jonathan begins, then, by naming Lou's death by suicide openly and honestly. He graphically describes the "bleakness of suicidal depression." He calls for empathy and compassion from the assembled grievers. He then connects Lou's story to the story of faith, naming the present Jewish season that marks the destruction of the Holy Temple in Jerusalem. He evokes Lamentations 1, describing it as:

> . . . not only the lament of a people for the loss of their holy city and sanctuary, but also the cry of the tormented individual lost in the hell of depression.

After connecting Lou's story to the scriptural story, the rabbi shares his own story:

> My father committed suicide in 1979. He was so miserable, so abandoned in the mazes of his own diseased mind, that he actually thought that his absence would be better for us than his presence. I mention my dad because I want Lou's family to know that I know of almost no one who has not been touched by a suicide. It is an astonishingly widespread cause of death.

The pastor, having intersected his story with Lou and Lou's family's stories, connects with the stories of the assembled grievers:

And so I ask all of us gathered here: who here has a relative who took his or her own life?

(Many hands were raised.) The rabbi continues with a strategy for addressing the particular grief challenges for loved ones of suicide victims:

Let's end the secrecy and just talk about it together, in all of its confusion and strangeness. Let's weep about it together. For reasons that are beyond our grasp, it is hard to be a human being. Some of us simply cannot make it through the entire journey and gauntlet of life.

He addresses Lou's children directly:

When my daughters were younger and asked why their grandfather Samuel was not alive, I decided not to lie. I told them he had a "sadness disease"—not the regular kind of sadness that everyone knows, in which, even at its worst, a small part of you knows that it will pass away like a rain cloud and that more pleasant moods will return, but a kind of sadness that never goes away. Lou had the sadness disease. Some people recover. But some people die from the disease, like my father did, and now like your father. It doesn't mean Lou didn't love you. I think you know how much your dad loved you, just like I know how much my dad loved me.

The rabbi continues, acknowledging and giving permission for the grievers' emotions:

I was very angry with my dad for a long time. That is to be expected. Why did he abandon us? But as the anger subsided, and as I could begin to imagine what life must have been like for him, what remained was sadness for him. It is very, very sad that Lou couldn't recover and go on living. I know how much you are going to miss him.

The rabbi then helps Lou's family create a future story—one that will be cocreated with the assembled congregation. He helps Lou's family begin a new relationship with Lou, one based on memory, legacy, and love:

I love you, as do many, many people, a lot of whom are here right now, and we want to keep you company and make life good and sweet for you even though your dad is gone. But he may visit you when you dream. I love when I dream about my dad. And I know that even though he is no longer here to hug me, his love is truly forever. As the Song of Songs says, "Love is stronger than death."

The rabbi then turns to Lou's life story, affirming that his tragic death will not have the final word:

I know that many of us here were touched by his generosity, thoughtfulness, and kindness. And what an intelligent man! And stubborn! And what a hard-working and determined man, so dedicated to his family, to his community, and to the Jewish people. Today I have spoken of the tragedy of Lou's death so that it does not linger in the shadows, so that we can now go on and speak of his life and laugh and cry and remember and tell stories. Begin telling those stories after the burial, and don't stop. Remember and honor the memory of Harold Lou Ward.

The rabbi concludes his sermon by again evoking Lamentations so as to help the assembled grievers envision a hopeful future story:

We pass through it, we who survive the ravages of despair and find ourselves, sometimes to our own surprise and amazement, singing more hopeful songs. All you who mourn, if you happen to find yourself enjoying the splash of cold water on your face or the taste of good food or a sweet moment, breeze, or deep breath, do not feel guilty that pleasure is yours. Life is complicated and confounding, but it is also very good. Our loved ones, even those who are no longer here, want us to be happy. Even the book of Lamentations, which is the darkest book of the Bible, ends with a prayer of hope: bring us back, dear God, and we will return. Renew our days as in earlier times. I sing this prayer, and we sing this prayer, for all those gripped by that internal darkness that makes death seem better than life. May they return to life and be renewed in hope.

Throughout, Rabbi Jonathan has protested the stigma of suicide, honored Lou's life, empathized with and instructed the grieving, and assured them, evoking his own story and Lamentations, that in God's loving presence, all have the promise of new life and hope.

3. Putting It All Together: Life Story, Death Story, and God's Story

The examples above are examples of ways in which pastors engage the deceased's death story and life story in relation to God's story. Here is a more complete sermon that weaves together all three stories. Notice how Pastor Tom re-presents Bertha as a child of God, framing her life and then her death through dementia in the context of encountering God "in the sound of sheer silence."

Sermon Example: The Sound in the Silence (1 Kings 19:11-12)

From the stories of the earliest church Mothers and Fathers there is a story about the richness of silence. It seems that one day the great bishop of Alexandria went out into the desert to visit a monastery. When he arrived, all the monks gathered around the oldest, most respected member of the order and said, "Say a word to the bishop so that his soul may be benefited here." The old man replied, "If he is not inspired by my silence, he will not be inspired by my words either."

Our gathering this afternoon is for the worship of the God Elijah knew in that "sound of sheer silence" or that "still, small voice." We are here to worship God and to remember God's servant Bertha Rosemund.

She was a farm girl. Indeed, the stories of her life include a move with her family from Jacksboro to Abilene (a distance of well over a hundred miles) in a covered wagon when she was three years old. Then, when she was ten, she took a similar journey all the way up into the panhandle. She was a child who rode horses and lived in a place little more than a shack.

When she was grown, she took herself to Dallas and then to Fort Worth. During the war, she was a riveter at the bomber plant out on the west side. (Husband Rick Rosemund likes to say she could've been known as Rosie the Riveter if they had been married back then.) Later, she worked for Barrett's Jewelers downtown.

Rick was the good-looking young fellow who would give her a ride downtown, saving her the bus fare. A couple of years later, they were married, in December 1949. Then Rick Jr. came along. [The pastor appreciatively summarizes their family life.]

111

Bertha's life seems to have been full and good, although I know there were times of emptiness and want and mistakes and sins and all the rest. I trust that most of you are here because you remember her laughter or her words of friendship or of love.

I have to admit, I did not know any of that. For the Bertha Rosemund I knew was a woman of silence. It was neither her fault nor her intention, I know. But throughout the time I knew her, she was afflicted with a dementia that took away much of who she was.

I remember her in the narthex of the church, with a polite smile and a perplexed look at being introduced to someone called "the new minister." When I went to their home, Mr. Rosemund and I and the caretaker would talk. Mrs. Rosemund was silent. I remember, though, the love and the caring that were always in Mr. Rosemund's voice and attitude whenever he addressed her. Still, I don't think she ever spoke in my presence. Then when I hurried to her on her deathbed last Tuesday, she was already gone. I knew there was much that I had missed.

The tragedy and the disappointment and the sheer difficulty of dealing with such diseases can be awfully tough. When we come to a day such as this, we might be looking back with all sorts of regret. But it all depends on what you're looking for. [He tells the story of a farm boy hearing a cricket in the urban noise of Times Square. When asked how he could hear it, he said, "It all depends on what you're listening for."]

Moses knew God in the voice that roared in the fire of the burning bush and in the thunder on the top of Mount Sinai. But Elijah was different. Elijah knew God, but not in the earthquake or in the fire. Elijah knew God in "the sound of sheer silence."

What is it that we are looking for when we are with one whom we love? What is it that we are looking for when we encounter anyone or when we speak of someone's life when that person has died?

The things that count—the love, the mothering, the caring of a wife, the looks of admiration and affirmation, the help we know when times are tough—come even in the silence.

For that we give thanks and remember the epiphanies of holiness we have known in Bertha. Amen.

Chapter 7

Following Up with Grievers

The pre-funeral meetings (chapter 4), funeral services (chapter 5), and funeral sermon (chapter 6) may be over, but the funeral process is not. Though grieving is underway, grievers are still working on their tasks of grieving. The life story of their loved one has ended. They face the challenge of reconstructing their own life stories without the deceased's presence. The pastor and the congregation can play a crucial role in helping grievers negotiate these tasks of grieving and make new meaning of their lives after their life stories have been interrupted by this death.

Understanding current grief theories and the ways that they might usefully guide ministry with grieving people can help a pastor be effective in assisting ongoing grief work. Given the demands and responsibilities that pastors face, it is also necessary to have realistic strategies for effective ways to support the grieving in ways that involve not only the pastor but also the congregation.

Accordingly, this chapter has two sections. The first section outlines some changing understandings about grief that are emerging from recent research. The second section elaborates on five pastoral practices that the pastor can use in following up with grievers after the funeral service. These include helping grievers make meaning, helping grievers feel more secure in the love of God, helping grievers connect to deceased loved ones, helping grievers grieve while simultaneously creating new life, and helping grievers accomplish the five tasks.

By attending to the grieving in intentional and caring ways, the pastor, working with a congregation, can help grievers accomplish the tasks of grieving, experience God's loving presence, and create positive future stories of hope.

1. Significant Developments in Recent Grief Work

Pastors have long known "truisms" about grief. We may have said, or we have heard from others, that "time heals all wounds," that "God doesn't give us more than we can handle," and that the goal of grief is "closure." The latest research on grief indicates that much of what we believed to be true about grief is neither true nor helpful to grievers. Current research reveals that:

- *Grief does not unfold in predictable stages.* Elisabeth Kübler-Ross made significant contributions to the death awareness movement by identifying various dimensions of grief: denial, anger, bargaining, depression, and acceptance. But subsequent research indicates that grief does not unfold in these predictable, linear stages.

- *There is no normal way to grieve.* Some grievers may feel deep sadness. Some may feel relief that long-term suffering has ended. Some may feel joy, pride, and gratitude in recalling the deceased. Some feel relief or release given that they no longer must deal with the person on a daily basis. Most often, grievers experience a range of emotions. Though there are commonalities to the human grief experience, there are as many individual ways to grieve as there are individuals who are grieving and relationships to be grieved.

- *The goal of grief work is not to get back to "normal."* The death of a significant loved one changes life for the griever in significant ways forever. Grievers will come to know a "new normal."

- *Grief does not have a specified timetable.* Just as there is no one way to grieve, there is no timetable for grieving. Grievers grieve in their own way and at their own speed.

- *Grief work is not an isolated process.* Grievers benefit from being in community with those who understand and support their grief process.

- *The main task of grief work is not detachment from the deceased.* If grievers had a good relationship with the loved one during life, they may benefit from staying emotionally connected to the deceased through memory, ongoing legacy, and love.

• *The central focus of grief work is not "closure."* Much current work recognizes meaning making as the central challenge of grief work. The ways in which grievers make meaning of the death and of their own life story help grievers create a hopeful future story.

With these changing understandings comes an emerging profile that recognizes the complexities of grief and its effect on grievers on many levels. This emerging profile indicates that:

• Grief is a normal, natural response to loss that feels anything other than normal or natural to the person experiencing it.

• Grief is as individual as the relationship it grieves.

• Grief is experienced emotionally. Grievers feel a cluster of emotions, such as anger, guilt, denial, despair, fear, sadness, confusion, hopelessness, and possibly relief, release, pride, and joy. Grief does not follow a predictable pattern of emotions.

• Grief often involves experiencing and reexperiencing or revisiting emotions and feelings. Grievers do not progress through linear, predictable defined stages.

• Especially in the context of traumatic death, grievers can feel strong emotions, including anger, fear, and helplessness. Grievers need people with whom they feel safe and can express these emotions. When grievers can express intense emotions verbally, it often reduces their need to express the emotions through destructive acting out.

• Grief can be experienced physically, such as in bodily aches and pains.

• Grief can be experienced cognitively with poor concentration and an inability to pay attention or remember details. A sense of disorganization, searching, yearning, and confusion is normal for grievers. A sense of disorganization precedes any ability to reorganize and begin to make sense of life without the deceased.

• Grief affects people socially. Grief can change social status from married to widow, from daughter or son to orphan, from one in a relationship to one who is alone. Depending on the relationship and circumstances, the griever's day-to-day relationships and levels of sociability can be greatly affected.

- Grief affects people spiritually. Grievers may feel anger at and disappointment in God for not saving their loved one but also may feel shame for having these feelings. Or they may be relieved that "God took her" and wonder if that is okay. At a time when folk need God's presence the most, they may feel it the least. Or grievers may feel God's loving presence and comfort in this time of need.

- Grief takes its own time. Grief does not follow a specific timetable.

- Grief is experienced individually. Some people like to talk and say things over and over again. Other people go silent. Grievers benefit from a companion who will accompany them in the individual way that they grieve.

- Grief often causes people to isolate and ruminate. They are often not able to reach out to ask for help when they need it. Grievers benefit from ones who reach out to them and enter their grief journey.

- Grief involves meaning making as grievers seek to find meaning in the loss, about the loss, and after the loss.

Though grief is experienced in various and multiple ways, this profile of grief indicates that there are commonalities in the human experience of grief. When pastors are aware of common misunderstandings and helpful understandings about grief, we are better able to support grievers during and beyond the funeral process.

2. A Pastor's Guide to Following Up with Grievers: Five Practices

Informing this profile are some insights emerging from research into the experience of grief. Here are five effective practices drawn from current research on grieving for pastors to employ with grieving people.

Helping with Making Meaning

Current grief understandings emphasize, as I have throughout this book, that grievers must integrate the meaning of the death with their own life story. In fact, a focus on meaning making is at the heart of current grief research. Robert A. Neimeyer, who is at the forefront of this emphasis, asserts that "meaning reconstruction is the central process in what we conventionally refer to as grieving."[1] Attention to the ways in which grievers make meaning in, about, and after the loss has a significant effect on the ways in which grievers compose their life stories after their loved one's death. Chaplain Lindell Anderson recognizes:

> Finding the meaning in our losses can be a struggle. Our view of God can shape our response to suffering. If we believe that God is more powerful than suffering, that suffering is not the final word on life, that God can bring good out of evil and life out of death, it enables us to look for the good in our losses. Facing a major loss often causes us to evaluate and revise our priorities, dreams, relationships, and goals. Some of the most profound lessons we learn in life come from our losses. However, pastors must avoid placing too much emphasis on getting "over a loss." With many losses people don't "get over" them, yet many do get through them, and reconcile themselves to living with the grief. Many people develop a new sense of appreciation for life. Though we carry the past with us, it doesn't have to hold us back.[2]

Although meaning making during and after times of suffering and loss is not easy, it is necessary as grievers integrate a loved one's death into their own life story.

By *life story*, I mean those events that make up our daily lives and the significance or meaning we attribute to them. As I described in chapter 1, a life story has a plot constituted by the events, characters, and settings of our lives that we weave together with connections, causes, and effects. It has recurring perspectives, values, and a worldview by which we connect and interpret experiences, making meaning of various events. These perspectives, values, and worldview are how we make sense of things or how we make meaning of our lives.

Melissa Kelley provides a helpful understanding of meaning:

> Meaning is the deep sense we make of things, the way we understand the world, how we articulate the overarching purpose or goal of our lives, the significance we seek in living, the core values by which we order our lives. Meaning also includes theological dimensions, such as how we understand God's activity in the world, God's feelings about and responses to us, and God's role in suffering. Meaning, including theological meaning, helps to create order, sense, and purpose out of what could otherwise seem random, nonsensical, disordered, or chaotic.[3]

In relation to grief, this means that grievers must make sense of the loved one's death and of their own life story after the significant interruption of death.

How do pastors help grievers make meaning? Recall Sonja's story in chapter 3. Sonja was nine months pregnant. She and her husband, Tom, eagerly anticipated the birth of their first baby, a daughter. Prior to this pregnancy, Sonja had two miscarriages. When Sonja went in for a routine prenatal checkup, the doctor discovered that her baby had died. In the months following the stillbirth, Sonja and Tom made meaning in different ways.

Tom was devastated over the death of his first daughter. He talked to the pastor several times, explaining his inability to understand why God would take his precious baby and not give her a chance to experience life. His meaning making centered on not being able to understand the reasons for his daughter's death. Yet he also was able to affirm his belief that God was a very present help in this, their time of trouble. Tom knew that God had gotten him and Sonja through difficult times in the past and that God would get them through this. Tom was able to accept the paradox of being able to draw strength from God without understanding this death. Thus, he was making meaning of the death of his baby while maintaining his life story lived out in God's good and loving presence.

But Tom felt helpless to comfort his grieving wife. He knew that they were grieving in different ways.[4] He feared that their different ways of grieving would cause irreparable distance between them.

Sonja was making meaning in a different way. Sonja wanted to believe in a loving, comforting God, but she was not experiencing God's presence in her grief. Rather, she interpreted the stillbirth as God's judgment and punishment. For their entire six-year marriage, Sonja had prayed to be pregnant. When pregnancy did not happen naturally, she and Tom endured expensive, and what they considered demeaning, fertility treatments. She experienced two miscarriages at sixteen and eighteen weeks before finally carrying this baby to full term. Sonja had interpreted her earlier infertility and miscarriages as proof that God did not see her as fit to be a mother. The stillbirth of her precious baby, Rebekah, confirmed Sonja's understanding of her own life story. She believed that God was punishing her for not being a good enough Christian, for being too selfish, for not tithing, and for not trusting God enough. This understanding of a punitive God had been a familiar theme in Sonja's life story. Thus, Sonja was making meaning out of the loss of her baby in terms of her existing meaning-making structures of her life story in ways that were accentuating the devastating pain of her grief.

Sonja's and Tom's stories demonstrate the critical role meaning making plays in grief. Sonja and Tom made meaning of Rebekah's death in different ways. Tom does not understand the baby's death and attributes it to mystery. He can accept this mystery, however, in the context of his life story that affirms God as a good and loving God whom he encounters as sustaining them in their grief. He is able to integrate Rebekah's death into his life story in a way that affirms God's loving presence and care. Tom's understanding of God helps secure his belief in a hopeful future for Sonja and Tom. He believes that they will be excellent parents and can envision adopting children in the future if pregnancy is not an option.

Sonja is making meaning of Rebekah's death in a way that limits the possibility of a hopeful future. She interprets the death in terms of her prevailing life story that God is punishing her because God does not represent a loving, hopeful presence in her life. How does her pastor help in the meaning-reconstruction process?

The pastor initiated a meeting with Sonja after the funeral and listened to her describe her grief experience. In meeting with Sonja, the pastor realized that the way Sonja was making meaning of her baby's death and of her own future was causing her to feel hopeless. The pastor realized that helping Sonja alter the way she was constructing meaning would take time and patience. He suggested to Sonja that they meet regularly as Sonja attempted to make sense of Rebekah's death. Sonja agreed.

In the early sessions, the pastor asked about Sonja's feelings about Rebekah's death. Sonja explained that since she was a little girl, she wanted to have three children. She and Tom had talked about their desire for children early on in their dating relationship; it was one of the things that attracted her to him. She talked about the disappointment in their early attempts to conceive and the frustration and expense of fertility treatments. She talked in detail about the experience of giving birth to Rebekah, knowing that her baby had already died. She spoke of the unfairness of having to go through the physical pain of giving birth to a baby she would not hear cry, would not hold to her breast to nurse. She talked about God's cruelty in "making me give birth to the death of my dreams." The pastor listened carefully, saying empathic words such as, "I can't imagine your pain"; "I hear that you are very angry with God"; and "This has been a long journey to where you never wanted to be." Sonja nodded, cried, and said how grateful she was to be heard and understood.

In subsequent sessions, the pastor suggested that Sonja close her eyes and notice what feelings she felt in her body associated with Rebekah's death. Sonja held her stomach and elaborated the pain and devastation she felt with

Rebekah's death, which also reminded her of her two previous miscarriages. She shared with her pastor the pain, shame, and sense of failure she felt in both of the miscarriages. She described the cramping, the fear, the desperate prayers to God for a healthy baby, prayers that resulted in three dead babies. "Obviously," Sonja said, "God does not think I'm fit to be a mother." The most emotionally significant part of these losses to Sonja was her conclusion that God would never let her be what she desired to be most—a mother. She felt furious with God.

Sonja also said she felt guilty for sharing her anger at God with her pastor. The pastor assured her that it was okay to be angry with God and that the Bible has plenty of examples. The pastor talked about the biblical genre of lament. They read together Psalms 22 and 69, Lamentations 1, and Job 3. Sonja had never known of laments in the Bible. The pastor suggested other lament psalms to read before her next session. In her next visit, Sonya reported to the pastor that she had read those the pastor had suggested several times and had felt comfort to know that she was not alone in her anger and sorrow before God. She also reported that God seemed to be a little less angry and distant but that those feelings came and went.

Throughout their meetings, the pastor shared God's love for Sonja, assuring her that God deeply loves her and her three babies, that God has not abandoned them, and that God has been with Sonja, caring for her throughout the fertility treatments, through the miscarriages, and through Rebekah's stillbirth. He prayed with Sonja that God would lead her and Tom into a hopeful future.

The pastor presented a different view of God than Sonja had experienced, in part because the pastor modeled compassion for Sonja and Tom. Though initially resisting the idea of this kind of God, she said she longed to experience God's love rather than God's judgment and punishment. Sonja agreed for the pastor to lead her through a guided meditation, one in which he painted the picture of Sonja being held in God's loving, caring presence.

Over time, Sonja shared with her pastor that her views of herself were changing. Upon the pastor's suggestion, Sonja and Tom had been meeting with Compassionate Friends, a group of other parents who had experienced miscarriage, stillbirth, and the death of children. Meeting with other parents helped Sonja feel less responsible for her losses. Sonja also said that her views of God were changing. Through the pastor's supportive, loving presence, she was starting to feel God's supportive, loving presence. After several months, the pastor asked what steps Sonja could take that would be healing now; Sonja said that she and Tom had made an appointment with the fertility clinic. They wanted to talk to their doctor about the chances of her carrying another baby to full term. She said she now felt strong enough to begin to look into possibilities.

If we view this situation through the lens of Melissa Kelley's work, we will see that the pastor did three things here. First, the pastor cared for Sonja's story. Sonja experienced profound loss in her and her husband's attempts to have children. Not only has she lost those who were to be her three beloved children, but also she has lost hopes and dreams. She lost a sense of herself as one who deserves to be a mother. And she lost any understanding of a loving, present God with whom she has a hopeful future. The pastor realized that Sonja's meaning-making system was constructed over many painful, disappointing years. Sonja would need to tell and retell her story numerous times before the painful narrative could change. In hearing, attending to, and understanding Sonja's grief, the pastor cared for Sonja's story.

The second thing the pastor did was expand Sonja's narrative and re-interpret meaning so that Sonja can live into a future of hope. Sonja made meaning of her losses in a way that fit with her understanding and experience of what she felt to be a punitive God. By using biblical laments, the pastor was able to affirm Sonja's experience and introduce new plot material with lament literature, including the laments' movement from grief to praise and thanksgiving to a loving, gracious God. Eugene Peterson says that lament

> grounds pastoral work in the painful, patient facing of suffering that is an unavoidable part of the task.... By rooting the pastor in a way of taking suffering seriously, it encourag es the "longsuffering" of pastoral work, gives meaning and dignity to the person who suffers, and leaves the healing up to God in Christ on the cross.[6]

The pastor has expanded Sonja's story. In doing so, he offered additional possibilities for a hopeful future story. Such meaning reconstruction takes time. Deconstructing and then reconstructing systems of belief is difficult, painstaking work. But it can be done, especially with the support of a caring pastor.

The third thing the pastor did, then, was to offer care and support throughout Sonja's meaning-making process. Kelley suggests that pastors can help grievers with meaning making by offering "consistency of care and consistency of message."[7] Consistency of care involves a pastor being accessible and responsible to the griever, but within well-defined and mutually agreed-upon limits. Consistency of message consists of naming God as a loving presence who beckons all to a hopeful future. By consistently caring for and seeing Sonja's story in the context of God's story, the pastor helped Sonja gradually shift her meaning-making system toward greater awareness and experience of God's love. By helping Sonja recognize that her story is set in the context of God's story of loving presence and hope, the pastor helped Sonja form a secure attachment to God. This is discussed more below.

If we view the situation through the lens of Robert Neimeyer's work, we will see that the pastor has done four things in his work with Sonja. The pastor assisted her in reconstructing her narrative by moving over a period of time through four conversational blocks, consisting of (1) "various *entry questions* to elicit a 'thick description' of the story of the death itself," (2) "several *experiencing* questions to foster a more emotional, sensory engagement with the loss," (3) "*explanation questions* that explicitly engage issues of meaning," and (4) a set of "*elaboration questions* to prompt further reflective processing of the implications of the loss for the [person's] present and future."[8] Examples of these questions are:

Entry Questions

- What do you recall about how you responded to the event at the time?

- How did your feelings about it change over time?

- Who were you as a person, developmentally, at the time of the loss?

Experiencing Questions

- Close your eyes and visualize a scene connected with your loss. Take a few moments to find the image. Who or what is in the focus of your attention? Who is in the periphery? What is happening? If you are in the picture, where are you placed?

- What feelings, if any, do you notice in your body as you vivify this loss?

- What was the most emotionally significant part of the experience to you?

Explanation Questions

- How did you make sense of the death or loss at that time?

- How do you interpret the loss now?

- What spiritual beliefs contributed to your adjustment to this loss? How were they affected by it, in turn?

- Are there ways in which this loss disrupted the continuity of your life story? How, across time, have you dealt with this?

Elaboration Questions

- How has this experience affected your view of yourself or your world?

- What lessons about loving has this person or this loss taught you?

- How would your life be different if this person had lived?

- Are there any steps that you could take that would be helpful or healing now?

A pastor, in working through entry, experiencing, explanation, and elaboration questions such as these, in one session or over time, can help grievers recognize the ways in which their meaning-making systems are changing to make sense of the death that has interrupted grievers' life stories.

Another way a pastor can help grievers recognize and, if necessary, reconstruct meaning-making systems is to encourage grievers to write their grief stories in a therapeutic journal. This involves the following steps:[9]

- Suggest that the griever focus on the death.

- Write about the aspects that are most difficult to acknowledge.

- Shift between the external event and the griever's deepest feelings and thoughts.

- Write for a short period of time (e.g., twenty minutes) each day over several days.

- Schedule a "transitional activity," such as having a cup of tea, between writing and returning to normal life.

- Have the griever read it aloud to the pastor in a grief session.

Neimeyer and Kelley offer ways for a pastor to care for grievers' stories and attend to their present ways of making meaning before companioning them as new meaning-making systems are created. By attending to a griever's meaning-making system and, when necessary, helping a griever reconstruct this meaning-making system through consistency of care and consistency of message of God's story of loving presence and hope, a pastor can positively affect a griever's future story. A related pastoral practice for grievers involves helping grievers feel secure in the love of God.

Helping Grievers Feel Secure in the Love of God

A second aspect of current grief understandings evokes attachment theory, which has long informed grief practices. Attachment theory recognizes that our relational experiences from the very beginning of our existence shape the ways that we make sense of the world and ourselves. It suggests that our earliest relationships with primary caregivers shape our "attachment styles," or, the ways we attach to others in relationships all through life. Grief researchers and clinicians suggest that attachment styles also affect the ways that people grieve. By understanding attachment styles, we can better understand why people grieve in different ways and with different outcomes.

Attachment theory claims that people's attachment styles are a result of their early relationship experiences with primary caregivers. If infants experienced a secure attachment to caregivers who were accessible enough and responsive enough to their needs, they felt more secure and able to explore the world. These people most likely grew up with a secure attachment style. If, however, infants experienced their primary caregivers as inaccessible and inconsistent in care, they developed more anxious or avoidant attachment styles that most likely have affected relationships with others, including relationships with God, throughout their lives.

Attachment theorists argue that the death of a significant other activates the attachment behavioral system. When a significant loved one dies, a griever experiences anxiety because that loved one functioned as a "safe haven against distress" and is no longer physically present.[10] When death permanently separates someone from a key attachment figure, the griever will likely feel deep anxiety and sadness. If the griever has an insecure attachment style, the death may have a greater effect, confirming a basic life story belief that the world is neither safe nor secure. Attachment theorists argue, then, that attachment styles provide a clue as to ways that grievers will deal with emotions when a significant loved one dies.

We see examples of attachment to God affecting Tom's grief responses in the story above. Although Tom had experienced disappointing losses in his wife's two miscarriages after extensive fertility treatment, he felt like God's loving presence had "gotten him through." His experience of God's comfort and care in the past gave him the assurance that God would care for him and his wife, Sonja, through the devastating stillbirth of their daughter, Rebekah. Tom trusts that God has plans for their family's future. Tom has a secure attachment to God. Tom formed this capacity for secure attachment from his mother and father, his earliest caregivers. Both were accessible and responsive to Tom in his early years. His parents were Tom's secure base from which he could explore the world and return to their safety and security. Tom assimilated his parents' view of a good and loving God. Indeed, Tom has experienced God's loving presence all of his life.

Sonja, however, did not seem to have a safe, loving, or consistent relationship with God. When she did sense God's presence, it felt punitive and condemning. God was not a safe haven, a loving presence, or a source of comfort. This view of God paralleled Sonja's early experiences with her parents. Sonja's mother was an alcoholic and was sometimes gone for weeks at a time, leaving Sonja in the care of her older sister. Sonja's father, also an alcoholic, struggled to keep jobs. When unemployed, he flew into fits of rage, occasionally hitting Sonja's mother and often punishing Sonja and her sister for seemingly small offenses. Sonja grew up trying to be perfect to avoid her father's anger, though she still fell short of his expectations. Neither Sonja's father nor her mother provided a secure, stable base from which to explore the world. Sonja's aunt took Sonja to church with her many Sundays, but Sonja struggled to believe in a loving, caring God. After two miscarriages and her recent stillbirth, Sonja believed that if there was a God, God was still punishing her for falling short of who she should be if she wanted to be a mother. Sonja took no comfort from God in her grief. The most comfort she received was in trying to avoid God. In the same way, she was withdrawing from her husband. She resented the comfort Tom was receiving from God, resisted and was offended by his offers to pray with her, and was distancing herself from him, wanting to be alone in her grief and despair.

As we can see, Sonja and Tom's attachment styles with God are similar to their attachment to their parents. Tom, who experienced an early secure attachment with his parents, has a more secure attachment to a loving God. Sonja, who experienced an insecure attachment to her parents, who were neither accessible nor responsive enough to meet her needs, developed an insecure, avoidant attachment to God.

It is important to note that a person's attachment style to God is not fixed. People can change and so can their attachment styles to God. People can develop a more secure attachment to a God who can then be understood to be loving, present, and offering a hopeful future. This is an important understanding when working with grievers. Pastoral psychotherapist Phillip Bennett suggests that when grievers view God as the ultimate secure base, they may deal more effectively with loss and separation. He says, "The secure base of God's love will not take away our losses but it can help us discover an abiding Presence that sustains us even in the midst of things that are passing."[11] Grievers who have a secure and positive attachment to God often feel God's loving presence and comfort even and especially in the devastation of grief.

How does her pastor help Sonja develop a more secure attachment to God?

Melissa Kelley suggests three ways that a pastor can offer companioning and care from an attachment perspective:[12]

First, her pastor offers understanding. By listening to Sonja and caring for her, the pastor understands Sonja's pain, which is deepened by feelings that God is punishing her for her unworthiness. Her pastor does not try to change Sonja's narrative until he has a sufficient understanding of the origins of the story, which may go back to her childhood and likely even generations before that. In the same way, Robert Carkhuff says that one of the most important goals in a helping relationship is to identify the reasons behind a person's feelings, asking, "What personal beliefs cause the helper to feel this way about the situation?"[13] By hearing and understanding Sonja, her pastor cares for her.

Second, her pastor offers acceptance. He knows that Sonja did not choose this attachment style. The attachment style that Sonja developed was a response to her parents, who were neither accessible enough nor responsive enough to her early needs. Sonja's insecure attachment to God and her understanding of God to be punitive, judgmental, and distant are also not of her choosing. The pastor helps by accepting and not judging Sonja's insecure connection to God. He does not say, "You must not think of God like that." He does not feel the need to defend God. The pastor does not attempt to do a quick fix by merely quoting Bible verses and expecting a transformation. The pastor accepts that a shift in the way that Sonja is attached to God will take time and the caring companionship of the pastor and congregation.

Third, as in the meaning-making approach, the pastor helps Sonja form a more secure attachment to God by offering consistency of care and consistency of message. Recall his use of lament psalms to affirm Sonja's protest against her circumstances. Again and again, the pastor affirmed God's love for Sonja. By using guided imagery, by using Sonja's name when reading aloud Psalm 139, the pastor helps Sonja incorporate God's love into her life story. The pastor also involves the congregation in embodying these messages of consistency of care and consistency of message. The congregation, by demonstrating loving acts of care to Sonja and other grievers, is the living body of Christ.

By being accessible and responsive to Sonja's needs during her grieving, the pastor represents God's loving, caring presence. The pastor and congregation can become a secure base from which Sonja can explore her world, a world that she increasingly feels is a safe and secure place in the care of our loving, caring God. But this shift in Sonja may take many years, and even then it may not happen fully, especially if there is more trauma in her life. So the pastor must take a long view and be prepared to be patient.

Helping Grievers Continue to Connect with Deceased Loved Ones

A third aspect of current grief understandings involves the "continuing bonds" theory. This approach recognizes the ongoing relationship that many grievers continue to have with their deceased loved ones. Rather than encouraging grievers to sever emotional bonds with the deceased, grief clinicians now see benefit in grievers being connected to their loved ones through memory, legacy, and love.

In the pastor's work with Sonja, Sonja expressed the ache of not having her baby. Sonja described the intense loneliness she felt in going home to the nursery, with freshly painted lavender walls and a dresser filled with carefully folded newborn baby girl clothes. While she was sitting in the rocking chair near the crib, Sonja's arms literally ached with emptiness. "Continuing bonds" research says that Sonja's grieving will be more effective if she continues to invest emotional energy toward Rebekah rather than trying to sever the relationship. How can the pastor encourage Sonja to experience continuing bonds with Rebekah?

When the pastor asked about her feelings of ongoing connection with Rebekah, Sonja was relieved. She wanted to stay connected to her baby. The pastor assured her that continued connection is a healthy practice. In asking Sonja how she thought she could connect with Rebekah, Sonja came up with the idea of holding a pillow and rocking in the rocking chair in Rebekah's nursery. Although she knew the pillow was not her baby, it helped her connect to Rebekah and express her feelings by talking and singing to Rebekah, crying, and pouring her heart out to God.

In further discussions, the pastor and Sonja brainstormed other ways to stay connected with Rebekah. These included:

- writing letters to Rebekah and keeping them in a special box,

- visiting Rebekah's grave,

- becoming involved in children's causes or grieving parents' causes in Rebekah's honor, and

- connecting with Rebekah through meditation and prayer.

By connecting to Rebekah through memory, legacy, and love, Sonja felt closer to Rebekah, closer to her husband, Tom, and closer to God. She also began to connect with her other two babies that she lost in miscarriage, though the connection was not as intense. Sonja felt hope that she and Tom would reunite with their three children in heaven someday. In the meantime, she had renewed hope that somehow she and Tom would have more children.

Helping Grievers Grieve While Simultaneously Creating New Life

A fourth aspect of current grief understandings involves the dual process model. This approach understands grieving as moving or oscillating between grieving the death, what is called a "loss orientation," and creating new life, what is called a "restoration orientation." Grief clinicians assert that grievers cope well when they continually switch focus between these two areas of focus. This backward/forward orientation may feel disorienting to grievers, but the process is natural and helpful. If grievers focus only on restoration, they may be denying the death. If they focus only on the loss, they do not engage the task of creating a new future without the deceased.

A pastor can help grievers engage in the dual process model by recognizing and affirming when they notice grievers doing both of these activities. Sonja's pastor was able to affirm Sonja's loss orientation and restoration orientation when Sonja cried over the ache in her arms in coming home from the hospital without Rebekah (loss orientation). Subsequently, Sonja sounded more hopeful as she started to talk about making an appointment at the fertility clinic (restoration orientation). When Sonja asked the pastor, "Do you think it's too soon to think about another baby?" the pastor affirmed Sonja and Tom's prayerful process and assured them that God is beckoning them toward a hopeful future.

Helping Grievers Accomplish the Tasks of Grieving

As I have noted, research shows that grievers benefit from attending to five tasks. These tasks are:

(1) to accept the reality of the death,

(2) to express grief around the death,

(3) to make meaning of the deceased's life and death,

(4) to adjust to a world in which the deceased is no longer physically present, and

(5) to redefine the relationship with the deceased in terms of memory, legacy, and love.

The four pastoral practices outlined above are ways of engaging all of these tasks. For example, helping grievers make meaning, which is the central work of grieving, embraces all five tasks. Helping grievers feel secure in the love of God embraces tasks 4 and 5 in particular. Moreover, the pastor's involvement with the grievers throughout the funeral process outlined in chapters 1 through 6 also assists grievers in engaging these tasks.

All of these practices assume that the pastor is in regular contact with grievers after the funeral. When the funeral service ends, the relatives depart, the cards and casseroles stop coming, and everyone goes on with their lives, grievers can feel isolated, alone, and bereft. They often are too mired in grief to reach out, even to those well-meaning folk at the funeral who said to "just call if you need anything." Pastoral contact is now crucial. But the pastor does not just make social calls. With these five tasks of grieving in mind, a pastor makes contact to be a companion, walking alongside grievers and listening to their stories as they grieve in their individual ways. The pastor offers consistency of care and consistency of message of God's loving presence. In addition, with these five tasks of grieving in mind, the pastor assesses how grievers are engaging these tasks. The pastor can then employ pastoral practices outlined in this chapter as appropriate.

Also helpful for this ongoing follow-up work is a "grief calendar." This calendar can be paper or electronic. In it, the pastor records the date of the death, significant details, grievers most affected by the death, and dates of ongoing contact. The pastor then makes reminders for follow-up care on significant days such as birthdays, anniversaries, and Mother's Day or Father's Day. It is also helpful for the pastor to have a list of all those who have died in a calendar year, along with contact information of grievers most affected.

The pastor can use this list to send notes of remembrance on holidays such as Thanksgiving, Christmas, and Easter.

Involving members of the congregation in this ongoing care is important. Chapter 1 discussed setting up systems and training volunteers so as to offer ongoing grief care. Such people need to be trained and have understanding of the sorts of skills outlined in this book. An excellent resource to help set up congregational care is *The Caring Congregation: How to Become One and Why It Matters* by Karen Lampe (Nashville: Abingdon Press, 2011).

There are further congregational dimensions to ongoing care. Suggestions include:

- Offer memorial services to remember and honor the deceased. These services can be held at traditional times, such as around Memorial Day, Veteran's Day, All Saints' Day, Thanksgiving, or Christmas. And, depending on the needs of grievers in the congregation, they can be held on other days as well, such as around Mother's Day or Father's Day. It is helpful in memorial services to involve grievers through meaningful rituals, such as the naming of the deceased, lighting candles for loved ones, singing of meaningful hymns, ringing of bells (both church bells and handbells), and reading of Scripture that names God's loving presence and hope.

- Establish grief groups, depending on the needs and size of the congregation. These groups can be pastor-led groups or mutual-help groups. An excellent resource for either group is *The Grief Care Kit* by Harold Ivan Smith (Kansas City: Beacon Hill Press, 2008). Also consider creating themed groups, depending on the needs of the congregation. Suggestions include a widow's group or a widower's group. These groups can also be open to members of the community. The key focus of the group is meaning making. An important means is story sharing, in which members share the story of the death, their life story as it was before, and their life story as they are reconstructing it in the wake of the death of a central character.

- Offer Sunday school classes that discuss grief. Reading and discussing books on grief and loss open up discussion about unresolved grief and loss in people's lives. See the suggested reading list for suggestions.

Conclusion

Both the pastor and the congregation play a crucial role in helping grievers negotiate the tasks of grieving and make new meaning of their lives after their life stories have been interrupted by the death of a significant loved one. This chapter suggested specific ways that a pastor can care for grievers after the funeral service. Pastors reach out to grievers to help them make meaning of the death. Pastors help grievers feel secure in the love of God. Pastors help grievers stay connected to deceased loved ones. Pastors help grievers oscillate between loss and restoration processes in their grief work. Pastors help by actively assessing and assisting grievers to accomplish the five tasks of grieving.

In carrying out these pastoral practices throughout the funeral process, pastors attend to and facilitate intersections among the stories of the deceased, the grievers, the congregation, and the pastor. The pastor sets all stories in the context of God's unfolding story—a story of loving presence and future hope. By manifesting God's loving presence and hope, the pastor has the holy task of companioning grievers as they make meaning of this death event and construct their own next chapters of their life stories beckoned by God's hope and held in God's love.

Appendix

To find a complete copy of the appendix online, search for *The Pastor's Practical Guide to Funerals* at abingdonpress.com.

Pastor's Contact Information Sheet for _____

Pastor's Funeral Home Communication Sheet

Memorial Service Template #1

Memorial Service Template #2

Funeral Service Template #1

Funeral Service Template #2

Funeral Service Template #3

Graveside Service Template #1

Graveside Service Template #2

Pastor's Grief Follow-up Care Sheet

Pastor's Contact Information Sheet for _____

Name	Relationship to Deceased	Contact Information

Pastor's Funeral Home Communication Sheet

• Will the service begin with a processional, or will the casket be placed in the church ahead of time?

> o If ahead of time, how far ahead?
>
> o Will the casket be opened or remain closed?

• Will the family be seated prior to the beginning of the service, or will they follow the casket up in procession?

• Will a pall be placed on the casket, or will the flower spray remain on?

> o If a pall is being used:
>
> > § Where in church will the placement take place?
> >
> > § At what point in the service will it be placed?
> >
> > § Will family assist with the placing of the pall, or will that be done by the funeral director?

• What is the estimated length of time of the service (so that an accurate estimated time of arrival at the cemetery may be provided).

• Will the clergyperson be taking his or her own vehicle to the cemetery, or would he or she prefer to be driven in the hearse or other vehicle provided by the funeral home?

• For the committal service at the grave site, would the clergyperson like to use:

	Yes	No
Earth	____	____
Sand	____	____
Water	____	____
Nothing	____	____
Other	_____	

Pastor's Funeral Home Communication Sheet, Continued

• What stipends/honoraria are to be provided?

	Name	Amount
Church	_____	_____
Clergyperson	_____	_____
Organist	_____	_____
Soloist	_____	_____
Sexton	_____	_____
Altar servers	_____	_____

• Share with funeral director as soon as possible, preferably at least twenty-four hours prior to the service.

With appreciation to John O. Mitchell IV, Funeral Director at Mitchell-Wiedefeld Funeral Home, Inc. and member of the National Funeral Director Association media team, for providing content.

Memorial Service Template #1

Component Part	Possible Elements	Notes
Gathering		
	Music	
Words of Grace		
Greeting		
Hymn or Song	E.g., "Precious Lord, Take My Hand"	
Prayer		
Psalm	E.g., Psalm 130	
Old Testament Lesson	E.g., Isaiah 40:1-8; Isaiah 40:28-31; Exodus 14:5-14, 19-31; Isaiah 55:1-3, 6-13	
Psalm	E.g., Psalm 23	
New Testament Lesson	E.g., 1 Corinthians 15; Revelation 21:1-7; Romans 8	
Psalm, Canticle, or Hymn	E.g., Psalm 43, 46, 121, 139; "O Love That Wilt Not Let Me Go"; "Abide with Me"; "Hymn of Promise"	
Gospel Lesson	E.g., John 11, 14; Luke 24:13-35	
Sermon		
Witness	Reading of the Obituary	

	Family and Friends Speak Thankfulness to God for the Deceased	
	Poem or Other Reading	
Hymn or Song	E.g., "Great Is Thy Faithfulness"; "Amazing Grace"; "How Great Thou Art"	
Creed or Affirmation of Faith	E.g., Apostles' Creed	
Prayer	E.g., Prayer of Thanksgiving	
Lord's Prayer		
Dismissal with Blessing		

Memorial Service Template #2

Component Part	Possible Elements	Notes
Sentences of Scripture	E.g., Romans 15:13; Psalm 46:1; Deuteronomy 33:27; Matthew 5:4; 2 Corinthians 1:3-4	
Prayer	E.g., Eternal God, our help in every time of trouble, send your Holy Spirit to comfort and strengthen us, that we may have hope of life eternal and trust in your goodness and mercy, through Jesus Christ our Lord. Amen.	
Hymn	E.g., "Precious Lord, Take My Hand"	
Psalm	E.g., Psalms 22, 23, 42, 46, 121, 30, 139	
Scripture Readings	E.g., Isaiah 43; Matthew 5:4; Luke 23:33, 39-43; John 11, 14:1-6; Romans 8, 14; 1 Corinthians 15; Revelation 21	
Sermon		
Words of Remembrance	Reading of the Obituary	
	Family and Friends Speak Thankfulness to God for the Deceased	

	Poem or Other Reading	
	Ritual That Honors the Deceased	
Prayer		
Dismissal/Blessing		

Funeral Service Template #1 (Adapted from *United Methodist Book of Worship*)

Component Part	Possible Elements	Notes
Gathering		
	Music	
	Carrying of the Coffin/Urn	
	Placing of the Pall	
Greeting		
Hymn or Song	E.g., "Precious Lord, Take My Hand"	
Prayer		
Psalm	E.g., Psalm 130	
Old Testament Lesson	E.g., Isaiah 40:1-8, 28-31; Exodus 14:5-14, 19-31; Isaiah 55:1-3, 6-13	
Psalm	E.g., Psalm 23	
New Testament Lesson	E.g., 1 Corinthians 15; Revelation 21:1-7; Romans 8	
Psalm, Canticle, or Hymn	E.g., Psalms 43, 46, 121, 139; "O Love That Wilt Not Let Me Go"; "Abide with Me"; "Hymn of Promise"	
Gospel Lesson	E.g., John 11, 14:1-6; Luke 24:13-35	
Sermon		

Witness	Reading of the Obituary	
	Family and Friends Speak Thankfulness to God for the Deceased	
	Poem or Other Reading	
Hymn or Song	E.g., "Great Is Thy Faithfulness"; "Amazing Grace"; "How Great Thou Art"	
Affirmation of Faith or Creed	E.g., Apostles' Creed	
Commendation	(If Committal is to conclude this service, this may be shortened.)	
Prayer	E.g., Prayer of Thanksgiving	
Communion		
Lord's Prayer		
Dismissal/Blessing		

Funeral Service Template #2 (Shorter Version of *UM Book of Worship*)

Component Part	Possible Elements	Notes
Gathering	Opening Words	
	Invocation	
	Music	
	Carrying of the Coffin/Urn	
	Placing of the Pall	
Prayer		
Psalm	E.g., Psalm 130	
Old Testament Lesson	E.g., Isaiah 40:1-8, 28-31; Exodus 14:5-14, 19-31; Isaiah 55:1-3, 6-13	
Psalm	E.g., Psalm 23	
New Testament Lesson	E.g., 1 Corinthians 15; Revelation 21:1-7; Romans 8	
Psalm, Canticle, or Hymn	E.g., Psalm 43, 46, 121, 139; "O Love That Wilt Not Let Me Go"; "Abide with Me"; "Hymn of Promise"	
Gospel Lesson	E.g., John 14:1-6; John 11; Luke 24:13-35	
Sermon		
Words of Remembrance	Reading of the Obituary	

Funeral Service Template #2 (Shorter Version of *UM Book of Worship*), Continued

	Family and Friends Speak Thankfulness to God for the Deceased	
	Poem or Other Reading	
	Ritual That Honors the Deceased	
Hymn or Song	E.g., "Great Is Thy Faithfulness"; "Amazing Grace"; "How Great Thou Art"	
Commendation	(If Committal is to conclude this service, this may be shortened.)	
Prayer	E.g., Prayer of Thanksgiving	
Lord's Prayer		
Dismissal with Blessing		

Funeral Service Template #3 (Adapted from *Presbyterian Book of Worship*)

Component Part	Possible Elements	Notes
Gathering	Opening Words	
Placing of the Pall	For as many of you as were baptized into Christ have clothed yourselves with Christ. In his/her baptism, _____ was clothed with Christ; in the day of Christ's coming, he/she shall be clothed with glory.	
Sentences of Scripture	E.g., Psalm 124:8; Romans 6:3-5; John 11:25-26	
Psalm or Hymn	E.g., Psalm 23	
Prayer	Eternal God, maker of heaven and earth: You formed us from the dust of the earth, and by your breath you gave us life. We glorify you. Jesus Christ, the resurrection and the life: You tasted death for all humanity, and by rising from the grave you opened the way to eternal life.	

	We praise you. Holy Spirit, author and giver of life: You are the comforter of all who sorrow, our sure confidence and everlasting hope. We worship you. Amen.	
Confession and Pardon		
Absolution		
Readings from Scripture	E.g., Isaiah 40, 43; Lamentations 3; Psalms 23, 42, 121, 130; John 11, 14:1-6; Romans 6:3-9, 8; 1 Corinthians 15	
Sermon		
Affirmation of Faith	E.g., Apostles' Creed	
Hymn	E.g., "Great Is Thy Faithfulness"; "Amazing Grace"; "How Great Thou Art"	
Prayer	Of Thanksgiving, Supplication, or Intercession	
Lord's Supper		
Lord's Prayer		
Commendation		
Blessing		
Procession		

Graveside Service Template #1 (Adapted from *UM Book of Worship*)

Component Part	Possible Elements	Notes
Greeting	In the midst of life, we are in death; from whom can we seek help? Our help is in the name of the Lord who made heaven and earth. God who raised Christ from the dead will give life to your mortal bodies also through the Spirit that dwells in you.	
Opening Prayers	O God, you have ordered this wonderful world and know all things in earth and in heaven. Give us such faith that by day and by night, at all times and in all places, we may without fear commit ourselves and those dear to us to your never-failing love, in this life and in the life to come. Amen.	
Scriptures	E.g., John 12:24-26	

Committal	Almighty God, into your hands we commend your son/daughter, _____, in sure and certain hope of resurrection to eternal life through Jesus Christ our Lord. Amen.	
	This body we commit to the ground (to the elements, to its resting place), earth to earth, ashes to ashes, dust to dust.	
	Blessed are the dead who die in the Lord. Yes, says the Spirit, they will rest from their labors for their deeds follow them.	
Closing Prayer	Gracious God, we thank you for those we love but see no more. Receive into your arms your servant, _____, and grant that increasing in knowledge and love of you, he/she may go from strength to strength in service to your heavenly kingdom; through Jesus Christ our Lord. Amen.	

Dismissal with Blessing	Now to the One who is able to keep you from falling and to make you stand without blemish in the presence of God's glory with rejoicing, to the only God our Savior, through Jesus Christ our Lord, be glory, majesty, power, and authority, before all time and now and forever. Amen.	

Graveside Service Template #2 (Adapted from *Presbyterian Book of Worship*)

Component Part	Possible Elements	Notes
Scripture Sentences	Christ is risen from the dead, trampling down death by death, and giving life to those in the tomb.	
Prayer	O God, who gave us birth, you are ever more ready to hear than we are to pray. You know our needs before we ask, and our ignorance in asking. Show us now your grace, that as we face the mystery of death,	
	we may see the light of eternity. Speak to us once more your solemn message of life and of death. Help us to live as those who are prepared to die. And when our days here are ended, enable us to die as those who go forth to live, so that living or dying, our life may be in Jesus Christ our risen Lord Amen.	

Graveside Service Template #2 (Adapted from *Presbyterian Book of Worship*), Continued

Committal	In sure and certain hope of the resurrection to eternal life, through our Lord Jesus Christ, we commend to almighty God our brother/sister, _____, and we commit his/her body to the ground, earth to earth, ashes to ashes, dust to dust.	
	Blessed are the dead who die in the Lord. They rest from their labors, and their works follow them.	
Prayers	The Lord's Prayer	
	God of all mercies and giver of all comfort: Look graciously, we pray, on those who mourn, that, casting all their care on you, they may know the consolation of your love; through Jesus Christ our Lord. Amen.	
Blessing	The grace of the Lord Jesus Christ, the love of God, and the communion of the Holy Spirit be with you all. Amen.	

Pastor's Grief Follow-up Care Sheet

Name of Deceased:

Date of Death:

Follow-up Visits:

(1)

(2)

(3)

(4)

Congregational Involvement in Grief Care:

Significant Days:

• Birthday:

• Wedding Anniversary:

• Easter:

• Thanksgiving:

• Christmas:

• Anniversary of Death:

Griever	Relationship	Contact Information

Notes

Chapter 1: Preparing for Death

1. Eugene H. Peterson, *The Pastor: A Memoir* (New York: HarperCollins, 2011), 309.

2. These tasks are informed by J. W. Worden, *Grief Counseling and Grief Therapy: A Handbook for the Mental Health Practitioner*, 4th ed. (New York: Springer Publishing Company, 2009). Worden names four tasks: "To Accept the Reality of the Loss, To Process the Pain of Grief, To Adjust to a World Without the Deceased, and To Find an Enduring Connection With the Deceased in the Midst of Embarking on a New Life."

3. Henri J. M. Nouwen, *The Wounded Healer: Ministry in Contemporary Society* (New York: Doubleday, 1979).

4. Henri J. M. Nouwen, *Our Greatest Gift: A Meditation on Dying and Caring* (New York: HarperCollins), 1994.

5. Thomas Lynch, *The Undertaking: Life Studies from the Dismal Trade* (New York: W.W. Norton & Co., 1997).

6. Alan D. Wolfelt, *Understanding Your Grief: Ten Essential Touchstones for Finding Hope and Healing in Your Heart* (Fort Collins, CO: Companion Press, 2003), 6.

7. Nicholas Wolterstorff, *Lament for a Son* (Grand Rapids: William B. Eerdmans Publishing Co., 1987, 2001), 38.

Chapter 2: Caring through Anticipated Death

1. This bill of rights was created at the workshop "The Terminally Ill Patient and the Helping Person," in Lansing, Michigan, sponsored by the

Southwestern Michigan In-service Education Council and conducted by Amelia Barbus (1975), Associate Professor of Nursing, Wayne State University.

2. This section is informed by Edwin H. Friedman, *Generation to Generation: Family Process in Church and Synagogue* (New York: The Guilford Press, 1985), 168–78.

3. This section is informed by Paul W. Pruyser, *The Minister as Diagnostician: Personal Problems in Pastoral Perspective* (Philadelphia: Westminster Press, 1976), 60–79.

4. Pruyser uses "vocation" as a theme. I'm suggesting "meaning" as being more appropriate for end-of-life conversations. See Pruyser, *Minister as Diagnostician*, 76–79.

Chapter 3 Caring through Sudden Death

1. Alan D. Wolfelt, "Exploring the Special Features of Sudden Death, Trauma Loss and Suicide Grief," seminar in Plano, Texas, April 4, 2012.

2. This discussion is informed by Therese A. Rando, *How to Go On Living When Someone You Love Dies* (New York: Bantam, 1988), 90–94.

3. Warren Jones, "The ABC Method of Crisis Management," *Mental Hygiene* (January 1968): 87–89.

4. See, for example, Howard W. Stone, *Crisis Counseling*, 3rd ed. (Minneapolis: Fortress Press, 2009), 25–52.

5. This section is informed by Pruyser, *Minister as Diagnostician*, 60–79.

6. Pruyser uses "vocation" as a theme. I'm suggesting "meaning" as being more appropriate for death and grieving. See Pruyser, *Minister as Diagnostician*, 76–79.

7. Logan C. Jones, "The Psalms of Lament and the Transformation of Sorrow," *The Journal of Pastoral Care & Counseling* 61, nos. 1–2 (Spring-Summer 2007): 47–58.

8. Walter Brueggemann, *Spirituality of the Psalms* (Minneapolis: Fortress Press, 2002).

9. Edward P. Wimberly, *African American Pastoral Care*, rev. ed. (Nashville: Abingdon Press, 2008), 7.

10. Ibid.

11. R. Esteban Montilla and Ferney Medina, *Pastoral Care and Counseling with Latino/as* (Minneapolis: Fortress, 2006). See also Sheryl A. Kujawa-Holbrook and Karen B. Montagno, eds., *Injustice and the Care of Souls: Taking Oppression Seriously in Pastoral Care* (Minneapolis: Fortress Press, 2009).

12. My thanks to Chaplain Khalebb Ramirez who shared this in personal communication, August 1, 2012.

13. This section is informed by David K. Switzer, *Pastoral Care Emergencies* (Minneapolis: Fortress Press, 2000), 118–33.

Chapter 4: Meeting with Family before the Funeral Service

1. Herbert Anderson and Edward Foley, *Mighty Stories, Dangerous Rituals: Weaving Together the Human and the Divine* (San Francisco: Jossey-Bass, 1998), 115. For similar perspectives around the chief function of the funeral being to benefit grievers, see Gene Fowler, *Caring through the Funeral: A Pastor's Guide* (St. Louis, MO: Chalice Press, 2004); Paul E. Iron, *The Funeral and the Mourners: Pastoral Care of the Bereaved* (New York and Nashville: Abingdon Press, 1954); Alan D. Wolfelt, *Creating Meaningful Funeral Ceremonies: A Guide for Caregivers* (Fort Collins, CO: Companion Press, 1994).

2. William H. Willimon, *Worship as Pastoral Care* (Nashville: Abingdon Press, 1979), 115.

3. Thomas G. Long, *Accompany Them with Singing: The Christian Funeral* (Louisville, KY: Westminster John Knox Press, 2009), xv–xvi.

4. Ibid., 137.

5. Kent Richmond, for example, recognizes that a funeral (1) satisfies the needs of the bereaved to do whatever they can for the dead; (2) emphasizes the reality of death; (3) provides a context for the expression of grief; (4) provides a place where friends and relatives can express and receive support; and (5) brings the hope of the resurrection to life. See Kent D. Richmond, *A Time to Die: A Handbook for Funeral Sermons* (Nashville: Abingdon Press, 1990), 28-32. This is consistent with W. A. Poovey, *Planning a Christian Funeral: A Minister's Guide* (Minneapolis: Augsburg Publishing House, 1978), 11–17.

6. Nouwen, *Wounded Healer*.

Chapter 5: Creating the Funeral Service

1. My thanks to chaplains Lindell Anderson and Robert Beltram and pastors Katherine Godby, Jim Gordon, Katie Hays, Tom Plumbley, Tom Reeder, and Ginger Watson, who provided answers to these questions.

Chapter 6: Creating the Funeral Sermon

1. Long, *Accompany Them with Singing*, 88–194. Willimon states that some personalization of a sermon should be used, "but long dissertations on the alleged virtues of the deceased are inappropriate at a Christian funeral because of our belief in the equality of death and our recognition that, at time of death, we hope not in our own virtues or deeds, but 'Our hope is in the name of the Lord'" (Willimon, *Worship as Pastoral Care*, 111). Paul Wilson says, "The sermon remains...first and foremost a proclamation of the gospel of Jesus Christ" (Paul Scott Wilson, *The Practice of Preaching* [Nashville: Abingdon Press, 1995], 287).

2. Kent Richmond argues that the funeral sermon "must provide an answer to three questions that are present in the minds of the bereaved: (1) Will the deceased be cared for? (2) Will the survivors be cared for? (3) What word does God speak in the face of death?" (see Richmond, *A Time to Die*, 50). Andy Langford argues that the funeral sermon has several foci: "1) The mystery, power, and promise of Christ's death and resurrection; 2) The life of the deceased in honest yet affirmative ways; 3) Comfort for the family and friends" (see Andy Langford, *Christian Funerals* [Nashville: Abingdon Press, 2010], 102).

3. I'm grateful to pastors Jeff Clayton, Mike Graves, Katherine Godby, James Gordon, Katie Hays, Meg Peery McLaughlin, Tom Plumbley, Tom Reeder, Holly McKissick, George Moore, and Ginger Watson and Rabbi Jonathan Kligler and Elder Linda King for their sermon contributions.

Chapter 7: Following Up with Grievers

1. Robert A. Neimeyer, "Meaning Reconstruction and Loss," in *Meaning Reconstruction & the Experience of Loss*, ed. Robert A. Neimeyer (Washington, DC: American Psychological Association, 2001), xii.

2. Personal conversation with Dr. Lindell Anderson, Board Certified Chaplain, August 6, 2012.

3. Melissa M. Kelley, *Grief: Contemporary Theory and the Practice of Ministry* (Minneapolis: Fortress Press, 2010), 77–78.

4. For a further discussion on different styles of grieving, see Terry L. Martin and Kenneth J. Doka, *Men Don't Cry—Women Do: Transcending Gender Stereotypes of Grief* (Philadelphia: Taylor and Francis, 2000).

5. Kelley, *Grief*, 90–92.

6. Eugene H. Peterson, *Five Smooth Stones for Pastoral Work* (Grand Rapids: William B. Eerdmans Publishing Co., 1992), 141.

7. Kelley, *Grief*, 92.

8. Robert A. Neimeyer, "From *Stage Follower* to *Stage Manager:* Contemporary Directions in Bereavement Care," in *Beyond Kübler-Ross: New Perspectives on Death, Dying and Grief*, ed. Kenneth J. Doka and Amy S. Tucci (Washington, DC: Hospice Foundation of America, 2011), 138.

9. Ibid., 139.

10. Emmanuelle Zech and Carrie Arnold, "Attachment and Coping with Bereavement: Implications for Therapeutic Interventions with the Insecurely Attached," in *Grief and Bereavement in Contemporary Society: Bridging Research and Practice*, ed. Robert A. Neimeyer, Darcy L. Harris, Howard R. Winokuer, and Gordon F. Thornton (New York, Routledge, 2011), 25, referencing John Bowlby, *Attachment and Loss*, vol. 1, *Attachment* (London: Hogarth Press) and John Bowlby, *A Secure Base: Clinical Applications of Attachment Theory* (London: Routledge, 1988).

11. Phillip Bennett, *Let Yourself Be Loved* (New York: Paulist Press, 1997), 31.

12. Kelley, *Grief*, 65–66.

13. Robert Carkhuff, *The Art of Helping*, 9th ed. (Amherst, MA: HRD Press, 2009), 130.

Suggested Reading

Chapter 1: Preparing for Death
Especially Helpful

Mitchell, K., and H. Anderson. 1983. *All Our Losses, All Our Griefs: Resources for Pastoral Care.* Philadelphia: Westminster Press.

Oates, W. E. 1997. *Grief, Transition, and Loss: A Pastor's Practical Guide.* Minneapolis: Fortress Press.

Regarding a Story-Centered Approach

Golemon, L. A., ed. 2010. *Living Our Story: Narrative Leadership and Congregational Culture.* Herndon, VA: The Alban Institute.

Regarding God's Story

Anderson, H., and E. Foley. 1998. *Mighty Stories, Dangerous Rituals: Weaving Together the Human and the Divine.* San Francisco: Jossey Bass.

Armistead, K. 1995. *God-Images in the Healing Process.* Minneapolis: Fortress Press.

Fowler, G. 2010. *The Ministry of Lament: Caring for the Bereaved.* St. Louis, MO: Chalice Press.

Concerning Grievers' Stories

Garrett, G. 2008. *Stories from the Edge: A Theology of Grief.* Louisville, KY: Westminster John Knox Press.

Kushner, H. S. 1981. *When Bad Things Happen to Good People.* New York: Anchor Books.

Weems, A. 1995. *Psalms of Lament.* Louisville, KY: Westminster John Knox Press.

Wolterstorff, N. 2001. *Lament for a Son.* Grand Rapids: William B. Eerdmans Publishing Co.

Concerning the Pastor's Story

Hester, R. L., and K. Walker-Jones. 2009. *Know Your Story and Lead with It: The Power of Narrative in Clergy Leadership*. Herndon, VA: The Alban Institute.

Jacobs, M. 2010. *A Clergy Guide to End-of-Life Issues*. Cleveland: The Pilgrim Press.

Lester, A. D. 1995. *Hope in Pastoral Care and Counseling*. Louisville, KY: Westminster John Knox Press.

Concerning the Congregation's Story

Lampe, K. 2011. *The Caring Congregation: How to Become One and Why It Matters*. Nashville: Abingdon Press.

Stone, H. 1991. *The Caring Church: A Guide for Lay Pastoral Care*. Minnesota: Augsburg Press.

Sunderland, R. 1993. *Getting through Grief: Caregiving by Congregations*. Nashville: Abingdon Press.

Chapter 2: Caring through Anticipated Death
Especially Helpful

Pennel, J. E., Jr. 2009. *The Gift of Presence: A Guide to Helping Those Who Suffer*. Nashville: Abingdon Press.

Other Suggestions

Evans, A. R. 2011. *Is God Still at the Bedside? The Medical, Ethical, and Pastoral Issues of Death and Dying*. Grand Rapids: William B. Eerdmans Publishing Co.

Hedtke, L., and J. Winslade. 2004. *Re-membering Lives: Conversations with the Dying and the Bereaved*. Amityville, NY: Baywood Publishing Company.

Kirkindoll, M. L. 2001. *The Hospital Visit: A Pastor's Guide*. Nashville: Abingdon Press.

Chapter 3: Caring through Sudden Death
Especially Helpful

Stone, H. W. 2009. *Crisis Counseling*. 3rd ed. Minneapolis: Fortress Press.

Wright, H. N. 2011. *The Complete Guide to Crisis and Trauma Counseling: What to Do and Say When It Matters Most!* Ventura, CA: Regal.

Concerning Death

Justice, W. G. 1982. *When Death Comes: A Handbook for Ministering to the Grieving*. Nashville: Broadman Press.

Meeks, B. G. 2002. *Standing in the Circle of Grief: Prayers and Liturgies for Death and Dying.* Nashville: Abingdon Press.
Switzer, D. K. 2000. *Pastoral Care Emergencies.* Minneapolis: Fortress Press.

Concerning Trauma
Cisney, J. S., and K. L. Ellers. 2009. *The First 48 Hours: Spiritual Caregivers as First Responders.* Nashville: Abingdon Press.
McBride, J. L. 1998. *Spiritual Crisis: Surviving Trauma to the Soul.* Binghamton, NY: The Haworth Pastoral Press.
Means, J. J. 2000. *Trauma and Evil: Healing the Wounded Soul.* Minneapolis: Fortress Press.
Wright, H. N., M. Woodley, and J. Woodley. 2008. *Surviving the Storms of Life: Finding Hope and Healing When Life Goes Wrong.* Grand Rapids: Revell.

Concerning Suicide
Kaplan, K. J., and M. B. Schwartz. 2008. *A Psychology of Hope: A Biblical Response to Tragedy and Suicide.* Grand Rapids: William B. Eerdmans Publishing Co.
Smith, H. I. 2007. *A Long-Shadowed Grief: Suicide and Its Aftermath.* Cambridge: Cowley Publications.

Concerning Cross-cultural Ministry
Kujawa-Holbrook, S. A., and K. B. Montagno, eds. 2009. *Injustice and the Care of Souls: Taking Oppression Seriously in Pastoral Care.* Minneapolis: Fortress Press.
Larty, R. 2003. *In Living Color: An Intercultural Approach to Pastor Care and Counseling.* New York: Jesssica Kingsley Publishers Ltd.
Montilla, R. E., and F. Medina. 2006. *Pastoral Care and Counseling with Latino/as.* Minneapolis: Fortress Press.
Wimberly, E. P. 2008. *African American Pastoral Care.* Rev. ed. Nashville: Abingdon Press.

Concerning Public Tragedy
Lattanzi-Light, M., and K. J. Doka, eds. 2003. *Living with Grief: Coping with Public Tragedy.* New York: Brunner-Routledge.

Chapter 4: Meeting with Family before the Funeral Service
Especially Helpful
McFarlane, D. M. 2008. *Funerals with Today's Families in Mind: A Handbook for Pastors.* Cleveland: The Pilgrim Press.
Purnell, D. 2003. *Conversation as Ministry: Stories and Strategies for Confident Caregiving.* Cleveland: The Pilgrim Press.

Concerning Family Systems

Culbertson, P. 2000. *Caring for God's People: Counseling and Christian Wholeness.* Minneapolis: Fortress Press.

Friedman, E. H. 1985. *Generation to Generation: Family Process in Church and Synagogue.* New York: The Guilford Press.

Richardson, R. W., 1995. *Family Ties That Bind: A Self-Help Guide to Change through Family of Origin Therapy.* Bellingham, WA: Self-Counsel Press.

Chapter 5: Creating the Funeral Service
Especially Helpful

Langford, A. 2010. *Christian Funerals.* Nashville: Abingdon Press.

Sheppy, P. 2003. *In Sure and Certain Hope: Liturgies, Prayers, and Readings for Funerals and Memorials.* Nashville: Abingdon Press.

Other Suggestions

Biddle, P. H., Jr. 1984. *A Funeral Manual.* Grand Rapids: William B. Eerdmans Publishing Co.

Danals, C. L. 2007. *Funeral Services.* Just in Time! Nashville: Abingdon Press.

Engle, P. E., ed. 1996. *Baker's Funeral Handbook: Resources for Pastors.* Grand Rapids: Baker Books.

Mansell, J. S. 1998. *The Funeral: A Pastor's Guide.* Nashville: Abingdon Press.

Chapter 6: Creating the Funeral Sermon
Especially Helpful

Richmond, D. 1990. *A Time to Die: A Handbook for Funeral Sermons.* Nashville: Abingdon Press.

Other Suggestions

Bregman, L. 2011. *Preaching Death: The Transformation of Christian Funeral Sermons.* Waco: Baylor University Press.

Hughes, R. G. 1985. *A Trumpet in Darkness: Preaching to Mourners.* Philadelphia: Fortress Press.

Chapter 7: Following Up with Grievers
Especially Helpful

Doka, K. J., and A. S. Tucci. 2011. *Beyond Kübler-Ross: New Perspectives on Death, Dying and Grief.* Washington, DC: Hospice Foundation of America.

Kelley, M. M. 2010. *Grief: Contemporary Theory and the Practice of Ministry.* Minneapolis: Fortress Press.

Changing Understandings about Grief

Neimeyer, R. A. 2001. *Meaning Reconstruction and the Experience of Loss.* Washington, DC: American Psychological Association.

Neimeyer, R. A., D. L. Harris, H. R. Winokuer, and G. F. Thornton. 2011. *Grief and Bereavement in Contemporary Society: Bridging Research and Practice.* New York: Routledge.

Stroebe, M. S., R. O. Hansson, H. Schut, and W. Stroebe. 2008. *Handbook of Bereavement Research and Practice: Advances in Theory and Intervention.* Washington, DC: American Psychological Association.

Concerning the Pastor

Smith, H. I. 2001. *When Your People Are Grieving: Leading in Times of Loss.* Kansas City, MO: Beacon Hill Press.

Concerning Grievers

Lewis, C. S. 1961. *A Grief Observed.* London: Faber.

Sittser, J. 2004. *A Grace Disguised: How the Soul Grows through Loss.* Grand Rapids: Zondervan.

VanDuivendyk, T.P. 2006. *The Unwanted Gift of Grief: A Ministry Approach.* Binghamton, N.Y: Haworth Pastoral Press.

Weaver, A. J., and H. W. Stone, eds. 2005. *Reflections on Grief and Spiritual Growth.* Nashville: Abingdon Press.

CPSIA information can be obtained
at www.ICGtesting.com
Printed in the USA
LVHW091716080819
626994LV00007B/1027/P

9 781426 758195